I0500490

Strain

Navigating the Turbulent Waters of Family Business Succession

Robert Jhonson

Preface

For over two decades I have navigated the world of family businesses, their celebrations and their heartaches. In the corridors of family businesses, a silent struggle unfolds—one that transcends balance sheets and profit margins. It is a narrative of pain and sacrifice, of dreams built and dreams deferred. This is the untold story of generational transition, a saga where founders pass the torch to heirs, and the torch, heavy with legacy, can either illuminate a path to prosperity or cast shadows that threaten the very foundations of familial bonds and business empires.

The statistics are stark, revealing a harsh reality: only a third of family businesses survive the journey to the second generation, and even fewer persevere into the third. Yet, behind these numbers lies a deeper truth—an unspoken agony that arises when the generational transition is not meticulously prepared for, when it becomes a tempest instead of a seamless evolution.

This book, "Strain: Navigating the Turbulent Waters of Family Business Succession," seeks to illuminate the nuances of this silent suffering, to unravel the intricacies of a process that extends far beyond a mere transfer of power. The generational transition is not a singular act but a protracted journey, a tapestry woven over years, sometimes decades.

As we embark on this exploration, we delve into the emotional landscape of founders reluctant to let go, of heirs grappling with the weight of expectations, and of families torn between preserving tradition and embracing the winds of change. Through the pages that follow, we confront the paradoxes of preparation, the chasms of communication, and the stumbling blocks that too often derail successions.

Drawing on real-world experiences, case studies, and expert insights, we navigate the uncharted waters of succession planning. From the preparation paradox to the emotional resilience required in farewells, we confront the challenges head-on, offering practical solutions and preemptive measures.

This book is a call to action—a call to break the cycle of silent suffering and pave a smoother path for the generations to come. Together, let us embark on a journey to understand, navigate, and ultimately triumph over the strains of generational transition in family businesses.

Robert Jhonson

Understanding the Evolution of Family Businesses

1.1 Historical Context of Family Businesses

To truly understand the dynamics of generational succession in family businesses, it is essential to explore their historical context. Family businesses have been a fundamental part of economies around the world for centuries, with their roots dating back to ancient civilizations.

Throughout history, family businesses have played a significant role in shaping economies, communities, and societies. They have been the backbone of many industries, from agriculture and manufacturing to retail and services. The longevity and resilience of family businesses can be attributed to their ability to adapt and evolve across generations.

In the early stages of human civilization, family businesses were the primary form of economic organization. Families worked together to cultivate land, produce goods, and trade with neighboring communities. These businesses were often passed down from one generation to the next, ensuring continuity and stability.

During the Industrial Revolution in the 18th and 19th centuries, family businesses faced significant challenges and opportunities. The advent of new technologies and the rise of industrialization transformed the economic landscape. Many family businesses had to adapt their traditional methods to keep up with the changing times. Some successfully transitioned into larger-scale operations, while others struggled to compete with emerging industries.

The 20th century witnessed further transformations in family businesses. The post-World War II era saw the rise of the baby boomer generation, which brought a wave of ambition and growth to family businesses. Many businesses expanded their operations, diversified their offerings, and embraced new management practices.

However, the latter half of the 20th century also marked a shift in societal values and expectations. The rise of individualism and the pursuit of personal fulfillment led to a decline in the number of individuals willing to continue the family business. This shift, coupled with the increasing complexity of business operations, posed new challenges for family businesses.

Today, family businesses continue to be a vital part of the global economy. They range from small, local enterprises to multinational corporations. Despite the challenges they face, family businesses have proven to be resilient and adaptable, leveraging their unique strengths to thrive in an ever-changing business landscape.

Understanding the historical context of family businesses provides valuable insights into their evolution and the challenges they face. It allows us to appreciate the rich heritage and legacy that family businesses carry, as well as the importance of navigating generational succession to ensure their continued success. In the following sections, we will explore the transformation across generations, the characteristics of family businesses, and the values and expectations of each generation involved in the family business.

1.2 Transformation Across Generations

The transformation of family businesses across generations is a fascinating and intricate process. It involves the passing down of knowledge, values, and responsibilities from one generation to the next, while also adapting to the changing business landscape and societal norms. This transformation is crucial for the long-term success and sustainability of family businesses.

1.2.1 Evolution of Family Businesses

Family businesses have been a cornerstone of economies throughout history. They have evolved and adapted to various economic, social, and technological changes over time. Understanding the historical context of family businesses provides valuable insights into their transformation across generations.

In the early stages, family businesses were often small-scale operations, with family members working together to meet the needs of their community. As societies developed and economies grew, family businesses expanded their operations and became more complex. The industrial revolution brought about significant changes, as family businesses had to adapt to new technologies and production methods.

The transformation of family businesses continued into the 20th century, with the rise of multinational corporations and globalization. Many family businesses faced challenges in competing with larger, more established companies. However, some family businesses thrived by leveraging their unique strengths, such as their ability to make quick decisions and maintain strong relationships with customers.

1.2.2 Adaptation to Changing Times

One of the key aspects of transformation across generations is the ability of family businesses to adapt to changing times. Each generation brings its own set of skills, perspectives, and ideas, which can contribute to the growth and evolution of the business.

The younger generation often brings fresh ideas and a willingness to embrace new technologies and business practices. They may introduce innovative strategies, such as digital marketing or e-commerce, to expand the business's reach and competitiveness. This adaptability is crucial in today's rapidly changing business landscape, where technological advancements and shifting consumer preferences can greatly impact the success of a business.

However, it is also important for family businesses to strike a balance between embracing change and preserving the core values and traditions that have made the business successful. The older generation, with their wealth of experience and knowledge, can provide valuable guidance and mentorship to the younger generation. By combining the wisdom of the older generation with the innovative ideas of the younger generation, family businesses can navigate the challenges of transformation and ensure long-term success.

1.2.3 Legacy and Continuity

Another important aspect of transformation across generations is the preservation of the family business's legacy and continuity. Family businesses often have a strong sense of identity and purpose, which is deeply rooted in their history and values. It is essential to maintain this sense of identity while also adapting to the changing needs and expectations of customers and the market.

Succession planning plays a crucial role in ensuring the smooth transition of leadership and decision-making from one generation to the next. It involves identifying and preparing the next generation of leaders, establishing clear roles and responsibilities, and fostering open communication and collaboration between generations. By actively involving the younger generation in the decision-making process and providing them with opportunities to develop their skills and knowledge, family businesses can ensure a seamless transition and maintain continuity.

In conclusion, the transformation of family businesses across generations is a complex and dynamic process. It involves adapting to changing times, embracing innovation, and preserving the core values and legacy of the business. By understanding the historical context, characteristics, and expectations of each generation, family businesses can navigate the challenges of succession and ensure long-term success.

1.3 Characteristics of Family Businesses

Family businesses are unique entities that possess distinct characteristics that set them apart from other types of businesses. Understanding these characteristics is essential for effectively navigating generational succession and ensuring the long-term success of the business. In this section, we will explore some of the key characteristics of family businesses.

1.3.1 Long-Term Orientation

One of the defining characteristics of family businesses is their long-term orientation. Unlike publicly traded companies that often prioritize short-term profits, family businesses tend to focus on building a legacy that can be passed down through generations. This long-term perspective allows family businesses to make decisions that may not yield immediate financial gains but contribute to the sustainability and growth of the business over time.

1.3.2 Strong Family Identity

Family businesses are deeply rooted in the family's identity and values. The family's history, traditions, and shared experiences shape the culture and ethos of the business. This strong family identity often fosters a sense of loyalty, commitment, and pride among family members, which can be a significant asset in the success of the business.

1.3.3 Close-Knit Relationships

Family businesses are characterized by close-knit relationships among family members. These relationships are built on trust, mutual understanding, and shared experiences. The close proximity of family members within the business can create a unique dynamic, where personal and professional boundaries may blur. While this can foster a strong sense of camaraderie and collaboration, it can also lead to challenges when conflicts arise.

1.3.4 Informal Communication

In family businesses, communication often takes on an informal nature. Family members may rely on informal channels such as family gatherings, meals, or casual conversations to discuss business matters. This informal communication style can facilitate open and honest dialogue, allowing for quick decision-making and problem-solving. However, it can also lead to miscommunication or the exclusion of non-family employees from important discussions.

1.3.5 Dual Roles and Responsibilities

Family members in a family business often wear multiple hats, assuming both family and business roles simultaneously. This dual role can create unique challenges as family members navigate the complexities of family dynamics while also fulfilling their responsibilities within the business. Balancing these roles requires clear boundaries, effective communication, and a shared understanding of expectations.

1.3.6 Succession Planning

Family businesses typically have a strong focus on succession planning, as the transition of leadership and ownership from one generation to the next is a critical milestone. Succession planning involves identifying and preparing the next generation of leaders, ensuring a smooth and seamless transfer of power. It requires careful consideration of family dynamics, individual capabilities, and the long-term vision of the business.

1.3.7 Commitment to the Community

Family businesses often have a deep commitment to the communities in which they operate. This commitment stems from a sense of responsibility and a desire to contribute positively to society. Family businesses may engage in philanthropic activities, support local initiatives, or prioritize sustainable business practices. This commitment to the community not only enhances the reputation of the business but also strengthens the bond between the business and its stakeholders.

Understanding the unique characteristics of family businesses is crucial for effectively managing generational succession. By recognizing and leveraging these characteristics, family businesses can navigate the complexities of succession planning, resolve conflicts, and ensure the long-term success and sustainability of the business.

1.4 Values and Expectations of Each Generation

Understanding the values and expectations of each generation is essential for fostering effective communication, collaboration, and harmony within a family business. Each generation brings its unique perspectives, experiences, and priorities to the table, which can significantly impact the dynamics of the business. By recognizing and appreciating these differences, family businesses can leverage the strengths of each generation and create a cohesive and successful environment.

1.4.1 The Silent Generation: Tradition and Stability

The Silent Generation, born between 1925 and 1945, grew up during a time of economic instability and war. As a result, they value tradition, stability, and loyalty. They tend to be hardworking, disciplined, and risk averse. The Silent Generation often prioritizes the preservation of the family legacy and the continuation of established practices. They value hierarchy and respect for authority, and they expect loyalty and commitment from their successors.

1.4.2 Baby Boomers: Ambition and Growth

Baby Boomers, born between 1946 and 1964, experienced a period of economic prosperity and social change. They are known for their ambition, work ethic, and desire for growth. Baby Boomers often prioritize financial success and expansion. They value hard work, dedication, and loyalty. They expect their successors to demonstrate a strong commitment to the business and to continue driving growth and innovation.

1.4.3 Generation X: Independence and Adaptability

Generation X, born between 1965 and 1980, witnessed significant technological advancements and societal shifts. They value independence, adaptability, and work-life balance. Generation X tends to be pragmatic, self-reliant, and flexible. They prioritize personal fulfillment and seek a healthy balance between work and personal life. Generation X expects their successors to demonstrate competence, independence, and the ability to adapt to changing market conditions.

1.4.4 Millennials: Innovation and Collaboration

Millennials, born between 1981 and 1996, grew up in the digital age and are known for their tech-savviness, innovation, and collaboration. They value purpose, social responsibility, and work-life integration. Millennials prioritize meaningful work, personal development, and a positive impact on society. They expect their successors to embrace technology, drive innovation, and foster a collaborative and inclusive work environment.

Understanding the values and expectations of each generation is crucial for effective succession planning and ensuring a smooth transition of power. By recognizing and respecting the unique perspectives and priorities of each generation, family businesses can create a harmonious environment that fosters collaboration, innovation, and long-term success.

In the next chapter, we will explore the generational archetypes in more detail, delving into the characteristics, strengths, and challenges associated with each generation. By gaining a deeper understanding of these archetypes, family businesses can navigate generational succession with greater insight and success.

Generational Archetypes in Family Businesses

2.1 The Silent Generation: Tradition and Stability

The Silent Generation grew up during a time of economic hardship and uncertainty. They witnessed the resilience and determination of their parents, who often had to make sacrifices to provide for their families. As a result, the Silent Generation developed a strong sense of tradition and stability.

In family businesses, the Silent Generation values continuity and preserving the legacy built by their predecessors. They prioritize stability and are often resistant to change, preferring to maintain established practices and processes. This generation values hard work, loyalty, and dedication, and they expect the same from their successors.

One of the key characteristics of the Silent Generation is their respect for authority and hierarchy. They believe in clear lines of authority and decision-making, often favoring a top-down approach. This can sometimes lead to challenges when transitioning power to the next generation, as they may be hesitant to relinquish control.

The Silent Generation also places a high emphasis on reputation and maintaining a good public image. They value professionalism and integrity, and they expect their successors to uphold these values. This generation tends to be cautious and risk-averse, preferring to make calculated decisions rather than taking bold risks.

When it comes to succession planning, the Silent Generation often prefers a gradual transition of power. They believe in grooming their successors over time, ensuring they have the necessary skills and experience to take on leadership roles. This generation values loyalty and may prioritize family members over external hires when it comes to succession.

To successfully navigate succession with the Silent Generation, it is important to understand and respect their values and traditions. Open and honest communication is key, as it allows for a better understanding of their expectations and concerns. It is also important to demonstrate a willingness to learn from their experiences and seek their guidance.

In conclusion, the Silent Generation brings a sense of tradition and stability to family businesses. Understanding their values and expectations is crucial for a smooth succession process. By fostering open communication and respecting their legacy, family businesses can successfully navigate the transition of power with the Silent Generation.

2.2 Baby boomer

In Chapter 2, we focus on the generational archetype of Baby Boomers. Born between the years 1946 and 1964, Baby Boomers have played a significant role in shaping the business landscape. This generation witnessed significant social, political, and technological changes, which influenced their values, ambitions, and approach to business.

2.2.1 Ambition and Growth

Baby Boomers are often characterized by their ambitious nature and desire for growth. Growing up in a time of economic prosperity, they were driven to achieve success and make a mark in their respective industries. Many Baby Boomers took over their family businesses or started their own ventures, driven by a strong work ethic and a determination to succeed.

This generation embraced the idea of the American Dream, valuing hard work, dedication, and financial success. They were willing to put in long hours and make sacrifices to achieve their goals. Baby Boomers were known for their competitive spirit and desire to outperform their peers, which often translated into a drive for business expansion and market dominance.

2.2.2 Adaptability and Change

While Baby Boomers were ambitious and growth-oriented, they also demonstrated a remarkable ability to adapt to changing circumstances. This generation witnessed significant technological advancements, such as the rise of computers and the internet, and they were quick to embrace these new tools to enhance their businesses.

Unlike the Silent Generation before them, Baby Boomers were more open to innovation and change. They recognized the importance of staying ahead of the curve and leveraging technology to improve efficiency, productivity, and competitiveness. This adaptability allowed many Baby Boomers to successfully navigate the shifting business landscape and remain relevant in their industries.

2.2.3 Leadership Style

Baby Boomers brought a unique leadership style to family businesses. They were often characterized as hands-on leaders who were heavily involved in day-to-day operations. This generation valued hierarchy and structure, and they believed in the importance of clear roles and responsibilities within the organization.

Baby Boomers were known for their strong leadership skills, decisiveness, and ability to make tough decisions. They were often seen as authoritative figures who commanded respect and loyalty from their employees. However, their leadership style was not without its challenges. Some Baby Boomers struggled with delegating tasks and empowering the next generation, which could create tension and hinder the succession process.

2.2.4 Succession Planning

As Baby Boomers approach retirement age, succession planning becomes a critical consideration for family businesses. This generation faced the challenge of passing on their legacy and ensuring the continuity of their businesses. Succession planning involves identifying and preparing the next generation of leaders, whether they are family members or non-family executives.

Baby Boomers recognized the importance of succession planning and took steps to groom their successors. They understood the need for a smooth transition of power and decision-making to maintain stability and ensure the long-term success of the business. However, the process of succession planning can be complex and emotionally charged, requiring open communication, trust, and a shared vision for the future.

In conclusion, Baby Boomers have made a significant impact on the world of family businesses. Their ambition, adaptability, and strong leadership skills have shaped the way businesses operate and grow. As they navigate the challenges of succession planning, it is crucial for Baby Boomers to embrace open communication, empower the next generation, and foster a shared vision for the future. By doing so, they can ensure a successful transition and leave a lasting legacy for generations to come.

2.3 Generation X

Generation X, born between the mid-1960s and early 1980s, is a generation that witnessed significant societal and technological changes. As the bridge between the Baby Boomers and Millennials, Generation X brings a unique set of characteristics and perspectives to the family business.

2.3.1 Independence and Adaptability

One of the defining traits of Generation X is their independence and adaptability. Growing up during a time of economic uncertainty and rapid technological advancements, they learned to be self-reliant and flexible. This independence often translates into a desire for autonomy and the ability to make their own decisions within the family business.

Generation X individuals value work-life balance and prioritize personal fulfillment. They are known for their entrepreneurial spirit and willingness to take risks. This generation is often characterized by their ability to adapt to change and embrace new technologies, making them valuable assets in navigating the evolving business landscape.

2.3.2 Balancing Tradition and Innovation

While Generation X is known for their adaptability, they also have a deep appreciation for tradition and stability. Having witnessed the successes and failures of previous generations, they understand the importance of preserving the family legacy and maintaining the core values that have guided the business.

At the same time, Generation X recognizes the need for innovation and staying ahead of the curve. They are open to exploring new ideas and approaches, leveraging technology to drive growth and efficiency. This ability to balance tradition and innovation makes them effective leaders in family businesses, as they can bridge the gap between the older and younger generations.

2.3.3 Collaborative Leadership

Generation X is often characterized by their collaborative leadership style. They value input from all stakeholders and seek consensus in decision-making. This approach fosters a sense of inclusivity and empowers employees to contribute their ideas and expertise.

In family businesses, Generation X leaders understand the importance of involving family members in the decision-making process. They strive to create a culture of open communication and transparency, ensuring that all voices are heard and respected. This collaborative leadership style not only strengthens family relationships but also drives innovation and growth within the business.

2.3.4 Navigating Succession Challenges

While Generation X brings many strengths to the table, they also face unique challenges when it comes to succession planning. As the "sandwich generation," they often find themselves caught between the needs of the older and younger generations. Balancing the expectations and aspirations of both sides can be a delicate task.

Generation X leaders must navigate the complexities of succession planning, ensuring a smooth transition of power while addressing the concerns and aspirations of all family members. Effective communication and transparency are key in managing these challenges, as they help build trust and foster a shared vision for the future.

In conclusion, Generation X plays a crucial role in the succession of family businesses. Their independence, adaptability, and collaborative leadership style make them well-equipped to navigate the complexities of generational succession. By balancing tradition and innovation, they can ensure the continuity and sustainability of the family business while embracing the opportunities presented by the changing business landscape.

2.4 millennial

In this section, we will focus on the millennial generation and their unique characteristics, values, and expectations in the context of family businesses. Millennials, also known as Generation Y, are individuals born between the early 1980s and the mid-1990s. They are the first generation to grow up fully immersed in the digital age, with technology playing a significant role in their lives.

2.4.1 The Millennial Mindset

Millennials bring a fresh perspective to family businesses, characterized by their innovative thinking and collaborative approach. They are known for their entrepreneurial spirit and desire to make a positive impact on the world. Unlike previous generations, millennials prioritize work-life balance and seek meaningful and fulfilling careers.

One key aspect of the millennial mindset is their emphasis on purpose-driven work. They are driven by a desire to align their personal values with their professional endeavors. Millennials are more likely to be attracted to businesses that have a clear mission and contribute to social and environmental causes. They value transparency, authenticity, and ethical practices in the workplace.

2.4.2 Embracing Technology

Growing up in the digital age, millennials are highly tech-savvy and comfortable with using technology in all aspects of their lives. They see technology as an enabler and a tool for innovation. In the context of family businesses, millennials can bring fresh ideas and perspectives on how to leverage technology to drive growth and efficiency.

Millennials are quick to adopt new technologies and are often early adopters of emerging trends. They understand the importance of staying ahead in a rapidly changing business landscape. Their familiarity with social media, digital marketing, and e-commerce can be invaluable in expanding the family business's reach and attracting a younger customer base.

2.4.3 Collaboration and Inclusion

Millennials value collaboration and inclusivity in the workplace. They thrive in environments that encourage teamwork, open communication, and diverse perspectives. In family businesses, millennials can bridge the gap between different generations by fostering a culture of collaboration and mutual respect.

They are open to learning from older generations and appreciate the wisdom and experience they bring. At the same time, millennials are not afraid to challenge traditional practices and suggest innovative solutions. Their ability to adapt quickly to change and embrace new ideas can be a valuable asset during the succession process.

2.4.4 Work-Life Integration

Work-life balance is a significant priority for millennials. They seek flexibility in their work arrangements and value the ability to pursue personal interests alongside their professional responsibilities. Family businesses that can offer a healthy work-life integration are more likely to attract and retain millennial talent.

Millennials prioritize personal growth and development, seeking opportunities for continuous learning and skill enhancement. They appreciate employers who invest in their professional development and provide a supportive and nurturing work environment.

2.4.5 Communication and Feedback

Effective communication is crucial when working with millennials. They value open and transparent communication channels, where their opinions and ideas are heard and valued. Regular feedback and recognition are essential for their motivation and engagement.

Family businesses can create a culture of open communication by establishing regular check-ins, team meetings, and feedback sessions. Millennials appreciate constructive feedback and opportunities for growth. By fostering a culture of continuous learning and improvement, family businesses can harness the potential of millennials and create a harmonious succession process.

In conclusion, millennials bring a unique set of characteristics, values, and expectations to family businesses. Their innovative thinking, collaborative approach, and tech-savviness can be leveraged to drive growth and adapt to the changing business landscape. By understanding and embracing the millennial mindset, family businesses can navigate generational succession successfully and ensure a harmonious transition of power and decision-making.

Navigating Generational Conflict

3.1 Understanding Generational Clash of Values

One of the key factors that contribute to generational conflict in family businesses is the clash of values. Each generation brings with them their own set of values, shaped by the social, economic, and cultural context in which they grew up. These values influence their attitudes, beliefs, and behaviors, and when they differ significantly from those of other generations, conflicts can arise.

3.1.1 Values and Beliefs

Values are deeply held beliefs and principles that guide individuals' actions and decisions. They are shaped by a variety of factors, including upbringing, education, and life experiences. In the context of family businesses, values play a significant role in shaping the culture and direction of the business.

Each generation has its own set of values that may differ from those of other generations. For example, the Silent Generation, born between 1925 and 1945, often values tradition, stability, and loyalty. They may prioritize maintaining the family legacy and preserving the status quo. On the other hand, Millennials, born between 1981 and 1996, tend to value innovation, collaboration, and work-life balance. They may be more open to change and eager to embrace new technologies.

3.1.2 Conflicting Priorities

Generational clash of values often arises from conflicting priorities. Different generations may have different ideas about what is important for the business and how it should be run. For example, the older generation may prioritize stability and long-term sustainability, while the younger generation may be more focused on growth and innovation.

These conflicting priorities can lead to disagreements and tensions within the family business. The older generation may feel resistant to change and reluctant to adopt new technologies or strategies, while the younger generation may feel frustrated by what they perceive as outdated practices and a lack of adaptability.

3.1.3 Communication and Understanding
Effective communication and understanding are essential for bridging the generational divide and resolving conflicts. It is important for family members from different generations to engage in open and honest dialogue, actively listening to each other's perspectives and seeking common ground.

Creating a safe and inclusive space for communication is crucial. This can be achieved through regular family meetings, where all generations have the opportunity to express their thoughts and concerns. It is important to foster an environment of respect and empathy, where each generation feels heard and valued.

3.1.4 Embracing Diversity
Recognizing and embracing the diversity of values within the family business is key to navigating generational clash. Each generation brings unique strengths and perspectives to the table, and by

leveraging these differences, the family business can thrive.

It is important to foster a culture of inclusivity and collaboration, where all generations are encouraged to contribute their ideas and insights. By valuing and respecting the contributions of each generation, the family business can harness the power of diversity and create a harmonious environment.

3.1.5 Seeking Professional Guidance

In some cases, resolving generational conflicts may require the assistance of a neutral third party, such as a family business consultant or mediator. These professionals can provide an objective perspective and help facilitate productive discussions and decision-making processes.

Seeking professional guidance can be particularly beneficial when conflicts become entrenched or when there is a lack of trust and communication within the family business. A skilled mediator can help family members navigate difficult conversations, identify common goals, and develop strategies for moving forward.

In conclusion, understanding the clash of values between generations is crucial for navigating generational conflict in family businesses. By recognizing and respecting the diverse values and beliefs of each generation, fostering open communication, and seeking professional guidance when necessary, family businesses can successfully bridge the generational divide and ensure a harmonious succession process.

3.2 Identifying Sources of Conflict

Conflict is an inevitable part of any organization, and family businesses are no exception. In fact, the unique dynamics of family businesses often amplify conflicts, particularly when it comes to generational succession. Identifying the sources of conflict is crucial in order to address and resolve them effectively. In this section, we will explore some common sources of conflict in family businesses.

3.2.1 Differences in Values and Expectations

One of the primary sources of conflict in family businesses is the differences in values and expectations between generations. Each generation brings its own set of values, shaped by the social, economic, and cultural context in which they grew up. These values influence their decision-making, work ethic, and overall approach to business.

For example, the older generation, often referred to as the Silent Generation or Traditionalists, may prioritize stability, tradition, and long-term planning. On the other hand, younger generations, such as Millennials, may value innovation, flexibility, and social impact. These differing values can lead to clashes in decision-making, strategic direction, and even day-to-day operations.

3.2.2 Communication Breakdown

Effective communication is essential for any organization, but it becomes even more critical in family businesses where personal relationships are intertwined with business dynamics. Communication breakdowns can occur due to a variety of reasons, including generational differences in communication styles, lack of transparency, and power struggles.

Generational gaps in communication styles can lead to misunderstandings and misinterpretations. For example, older generations may prefer face-to-face communication or phone calls, while younger generations may rely more on digital communication channels such as email or instant messaging. These differences can create barriers and hinder effective communication.

Furthermore, a lack of transparency in decision-making processes can breed resentment and mistrust among family members. When certain family members feel excluded or uninformed about important business matters, it can lead to conflicts and a breakdown in communication.

Power struggles within the family can also contribute to communication breakdowns. When family members vie for control or influence, they may withhold information or manipulate communication channels to serve their own interests. This can create a toxic environment and hinder effective communication and collaboration.

3.2.3 Role Ambiguity and Conflict of Interest
In family businesses, role ambiguity and conflict of interest can be significant sources of conflict. Role ambiguity arises when family members have unclear or overlapping roles and responsibilities within the business. This can lead to confusion, inefficiency, and conflicts over decision-making authority.

Conflict of interest occurs when family members prioritize their personal interests over the best interests of the business. For example, a family member may push for a decision that benefits them personally, even if it is not in the best interest of the business as a whole. This can create tension and conflicts among family members, as they struggle to balance their personal and professional obligations.

3.2.4 Succession Planning and Leadership Transition

Succession planning and leadership transition are critical junctures in family businesses and can be significant sources of conflict. Determining who will take over the leadership of the business and how the transition will occur can be highly emotional and contentious.

Conflicts can arise when there is a lack of clarity or agreement on the succession plan. Different family members may have different expectations or aspirations for their role in the business, leading to power struggles and conflicts. Additionally, conflicts can emerge when the older generation is reluctant to let go of control or when the younger generation feels unprepared or undervalued.

3.2.5 Financial and Ownership Issues

Financial and ownership issues can also contribute to conflicts in family businesses. Disagreements over financial matters, such as profit distribution, reinvestment strategies, or compensation packages, can strain relationships and create tensions among family members.

Ownership issues, such as the distribution of shares or decision-making authority, can also lead to conflicts. Family members may have different opinions on how ownership should be structured or how decisions should be made, leading to disputes and power struggles.

Identifying these sources of conflict is the first step towards resolving them. By understanding the underlying causes, family businesses can implement strategies and processes to address conflicts effectively and foster a harmonious transition of power and decision-making.

3.3 Strategies for Bridging the Generational Divide

Bridging the generational divide in family businesses is essential for maintaining harmony and ensuring a successful transition of power. It requires a deep understanding of the values, expectations, and communication styles of each generation involved. In this section, we will explore strategies that can help bridge the generational divide and foster collaboration and understanding among family members.

3.3.1 Establishing Open and Transparent Communication Channels

Effective communication is the foundation for bridging the generational divide in family businesses. It is crucial to establish open and transparent communication channels that allow for the free flow of information and ideas. This can be achieved through regular family meetings, where all generations have the opportunity to express their thoughts, concerns, and aspirations.

Creating a safe and non-judgmental space for communication is essential. Encouraging active listening and empathy among family members can help foster understanding and bridge the generational gap. It is important to ensure that all voices are heard and respected, regardless of age or position within the business.

3.3.2 Embracing Diversity and Collaboration

Each generation brings unique perspectives, skills, and experiences to the table. Embracing this diversity and encouraging collaboration can lead to innovative solutions and a stronger family business. It is important to create opportunities for intergenerational collaboration, such as mentorship programs or cross-generational project teams.

By working together on common goals and projects, family members from different generations can learn from each other and develop a deeper understanding of their respective strengths and challenges. This can help break down stereotypes and bridge the generational divide.

3.3.3 Implementing Succession Planning and Development Programs

Succession planning is a critical component of bridging the generational divide in family businesses. It involves identifying and developing future leaders within the family, ensuring a smooth transition of power and decision-making. Implementing succession planning programs can help prepare the next generation for leadership roles and bridge the gap between generations.

These programs can include mentorship opportunities, leadership development workshops, and exposure to different aspects of the business. By investing in the development of the next generation, family businesses can ensure a seamless transition and build a strong foundation for future success.

3.3.4 Encouraging Continuous Learning and Adaptability

The business landscape is constantly evolving, and family businesses need to adapt to stay competitive. Encouraging continuous learning and adaptability among family members is crucial for bridging the generational divide. This can be achieved through ongoing training programs, industry conferences, and networking opportunities.

By embracing new technologies, trends, and business practices, family businesses can leverage the strengths of each generation and create a culture of innovation and growth. Encouraging a growth mindset and a willingness to embrace change can help bridge the generational divide and ensure the long-term success of the business.

3.3.5 Seeking External Expertise and Mediation

In some cases, bridging the generational divide may require external expertise and mediation. Family businesses can benefit from the guidance of consultants, coaches, or mediators who specialize in family business dynamics. These professionals can provide an objective perspective, facilitate difficult conversations, and help find common ground among family members.

Seeking external expertise can help family businesses navigate complex issues and ensure that the best interests of the business and the family are prioritized. It can also provide a neutral space for family members to express their concerns and work towards mutually beneficial solutions.

Bridging the generational divide in family businesses is a continuous process that requires ongoing effort and commitment from all family members. By implementing these strategies and fostering a culture of collaboration and understanding, family businesses can navigate succession successfully and ensure the long-term sustainability and prosperity of the business.

3.4 Resolving Conflicts in Family Businesses

Conflict is an inevitable part of any organization, and family businesses are no exception. In fact, the unique dynamics of family businesses often intensify conflicts, as personal relationships and emotions become intertwined with business decisions. Resolving conflicts in family businesses requires a delicate balance of understanding, communication, and compromise.

3.4.1 Understanding the Root Causes of Conflict

To effectively resolve conflicts in family businesses, it is essential to identify the root causes. Conflict in family businesses can arise from a variety of sources, including differences in values, goals, and communication styles. It can also stem from unresolved issues from the past or power struggles between family members.

One common source of conflict is the clash of generational values. Each generation brings its own set of values and expectations to the business, which can lead to disagreements and misunderstandings. For example, older generations may prioritize tradition and stability, while younger generations may emphasize innovation and change. Recognizing and understanding these differences is crucial in resolving conflicts.

Another source of conflict is the lack of clearly defined roles and responsibilities. When family members have overlapping roles or conflicting expectations, it can lead to confusion and tension. Establishing clear roles and responsibilities for each family member can help minimize conflicts and ensure everyone understands their contributions to the business.

3.4.2 Effective Communication and Conflict Resolution Strategies

Communication is key to resolving conflicts in family businesses. Open and honest communication allows family members to express their concerns, frustrations, and perspectives. It is important to create a safe and non-judgmental space where everyone feels heard and respected.

Active listening is a crucial component of effective communication. Family members should strive to understand each other's viewpoints and validate their feelings. This can help build empathy and foster a sense of understanding, which is essential for resolving conflicts.

In addition to effective communication, conflict resolution strategies can help family businesses navigate conflicts. One such strategy is mediation, where an impartial third party facilitates discussions and helps family members find common ground. Mediation can provide a neutral perspective and help family members explore creative solutions to their conflicts.

Another strategy is the use of family meetings or retreats. These gatherings provide an opportunity for open dialogue and problem-solving. Family members can discuss their concerns, share their visions for the business, and work together to find mutually beneficial solutions.

3.4.3 Seeking Professional Guidance

Resolving conflicts in family businesses can be challenging, especially when emotions run high. In some cases, seeking professional guidance can be beneficial. Family business consultants or therapists with expertise in family dynamics can provide valuable insights and strategies for conflict resolution.

These professionals can help facilitate difficult conversations, mediate conflicts, and provide guidance on effective communication and decision-making processes. They can also assist in developing a succession plan that addresses potential conflicts and ensures a smooth transition of power.

3.4.4 The Importance of Compromise and Collaboration

Resolving conflicts in family businesses often requires compromise and collaboration. Family members must be willing to find common ground and make concessions for the greater good of the business and family relationships. This may involve letting go of personal agendas and embracing a shared vision for the future.

Collaboration is also crucial in conflict resolution. By working together, family members can leverage their diverse skills and perspectives to find innovative solutions. Collaboration fosters a sense of unity and strengthens family bonds, ultimately leading to a more harmonious and successful family business.

In conclusion, resolving conflicts in family businesses is a complex process that requires understanding, effective communication, and a willingness to compromise. By identifying the root causes of conflict, employing conflict resolution strategies, seeking professional guidance when needed, and embracing compromise and collaboration, family businesses can navigate conflicts and ensure a smooth succession process.

Emotional impact

4.1 Understanding the Emotional Impact

Succession planning is not just a business strategy; it is a deeply personal and emotional journey for all parties involved. The process of passing the torch from one generation to the next can evoke a wide range of emotions, including joy, pride, fear, anxiety, and even grief. Understanding and acknowledging these emotions is crucial for a successful transition.

4.1.1 The Complexity of Emotions

Emotions play a significant role in family business succession, and they can often be complex and conflicting. For the current generation, the decision to step down and hand over the reins can be accompanied by a sense of loss, as they let go of a role that has defined their identity for years. They may also experience a mix of pride and anxiety, as they hope for the continued success of the business while worrying about its future under new leadership.

On the other hand, the next generation may feel a combination of excitement and pressure as they prepare to take on the responsibility of leading the family business. They may feel the weight of expectations from their parents, siblings, and other family members, as well as the need to prove themselves worthy of the opportunity.

4.1.2 The Impact on Family Dynamics

Succession can also have a profound impact on family dynamics. Sibling rivalries, power struggles, and unresolved conflicts can resurface during this time, adding an additional layer of complexity to the emotional landscape. The fear of disrupting family relationships and the potential for conflicts to escalate can create a significant amount of stress and tension.

Moreover, the emotional impact of succession extends beyond the immediate family. Employees, long-time business partners, and other stakeholders may also experience a range of emotions as they navigate the transition. It is essential to recognize and address these emotions to maintain healthy relationships and ensure a smooth succession process.

4.1.3 The Importance of Emotional Intelligence

Emotional intelligence, the ability to recognize and manage one's own emotions and those of others, is a crucial skill for all individuals involved in the succession process. Developing emotional intelligence allows individuals to navigate the emotional complexities of succession with empathy, understanding, and effective communication.

By fostering emotional intelligence, family members can create an environment that encourages open and honest conversations about their emotions, concerns, and aspirations. This level of emotional awareness and communication can help alleviate tension, build trust, and foster a sense of unity among family members.

4.1.4 Seeking Support and Guidance

Navigating the emotional impact of succession can be challenging, and it is essential to seek support and guidance throughout the process. Family business consultants, therapists, and mentors can provide valuable insights and tools to help individuals and families navigate the emotional challenges they may encounter.

Additionally, connecting with other families who have gone through similar experiences can offer a sense of validation and support. Sharing stories, lessons learned, and best practices can provide comfort and reassurance during this emotionally charged journey.

In the next section, we will explore the struggles of letting go and the emotional barriers that can hinder a smooth succession process. Understanding these challenges is crucial for both the current and next generations as they embark on this transformative journey.

4.2 The Struggles of Letting Go

Letting go is never easy, especially when it comes to passing the torch of a family business. For many business owners, their company is not just a source of income but a reflection of their identity, hard work, and dedication. The thought of relinquishing control and entrusting the business to the next generation can be overwhelming and emotionally challenging.

4.2.1 The Fear of Losing Control

One of the primary struggles faced by business owners during the succession process is the fear of losing control. After years of building and nurturing their business, it can be difficult to hand over the reins to someone else. The fear of the unknown, the fear of failure, and the fear of losing the legacy they have worked so hard to create can be paralyzing.

4.2.2 The Sense of Identity and Purpose

For many business owners, their work is not just a means to an end but a significant part of their identity and purpose in life. Letting go of the business means letting go of a part of themselves. It can be challenging to redefine one's identity and find a new sense of purpose beyond the business that has been their life's work.

4.2.3 The Emotional Attachment

Family businesses often have deep emotional ties. The business may have been passed down through generations, and the memories and experiences associated with it can be deeply ingrained in the family's history. Letting go of the business means letting go of those emotional attachments, which can be a painful and emotional process.

4.2.4 Trust and Confidence in the Next Generation

Another struggle faced by business owners is trusting that the next generation is capable of carrying on the legacy. It can be challenging to have confidence in their abilities and decision-making skills, especially if they have not had the same level of experience or exposure to the business. Building trust and confidence in the next generation is crucial for a successful transition.

4.2.5 Fear of Irrelevance

Letting go of the business can also bring about a fear of becoming irrelevant. Business owners may worry that without their active involvement, their opinions and expertise will no longer hold weight. They may fear being pushed aside or forgotten as the next generation takes charge. Overcoming this fear requires a shift in mindset and recognizing that their wisdom and guidance can still be valuable even in a different role.

4.2.6 Loss of Connection and Purpose

For many business owners, their work provides a sense of connection and purpose. It is not just about making money but about contributing to something greater than themselves. Letting go of the business can lead to a loss of that connection and purpose, leaving them feeling adrift and unsure of their place in the world. Finding new avenues for connection and purpose is essential for a smooth transition.

4.2.7 The Need for a Support System

Navigating the struggles of letting go requires a strong support system. Business owners need a network of trusted advisors, mentors, and peers who can provide guidance, reassurance, and a listening ear. Surrounding oneself with individuals who have gone through similar experiences can be invaluable in overcoming the emotional challenges of succession.

In conclusion, the struggles of letting go in family business succession are multifaceted and deeply emotional. Business owners face fears of losing control, a sense of identity and purpose, emotional attachments, trust in the next generation, fear of irrelevance, loss of connection and purpose, and the need for a support system. Recognizing and addressing these struggles is crucial for a successful transition and the preservation of the family business legacy.

4.3 The Weight of Expectations

Family business succession is not just about passing on leadership and ownership; it also carries with it a heavy burden of expectations. The expectations placed on the next generation can be overwhelming and can significantly impact their personal and professional lives. In this section, we will explore the various sources of these expectations and discuss strategies for managing and navigating them effectively.

4.3.1 The Family Legacy

One of the primary sources of expectations in family business succession is the family legacy. The previous generation has worked hard to build and establish the business, and there is often a strong desire to see it continue to thrive under the leadership of the next generation. The weight of carrying on the family name and preserving the legacy can create immense pressure on individuals, leading to feelings of inadequacy and self-doubt.

To manage these expectations, it is crucial for individuals to understand that they are not solely responsible for the success or failure of the family business. Succession is a collective effort that requires the support and collaboration of the entire family. Open and honest communication about expectations, goals, and aspirations can help alleviate some of the pressure and create a shared understanding of the path forward.

4.3.2 Personal Ambitions and Goals

In addition to the expectations associated with the family legacy, individuals involved in family business succession often face their own personal ambitions and goals. They may have dreams and aspirations that extend beyond the confines of the family business but feel obligated to prioritize the needs of the business and the family.

It is essential for individuals to recognize and honor their own ambitions while also considering the impact of their decisions on the family and the business. Finding a balance between personal fulfillment and the responsibilities of succession can be challenging, but it is crucial for long-term happiness and success. Open and transparent conversations with family members and trusted advisors can help individuals navigate this delicate balance and make informed decisions.

4.3.3 External Expectations

Beyond the internal expectations within the family, individuals involved in family business succession also face external expectations from stakeholders, employees, and the broader community. These external expectations can add an additional layer of pressure and scrutiny, making it even more challenging to navigate the succession process.

To manage external expectations, it is important for individuals to focus on their own values and priorities. By staying true to their vision and purpose, they can build a strong foundation for the future of the business. Seeking support from mentors, industry experts, and professional networks can also provide valuable guidance and perspective during this time.

4.3.4 Managing Expectations Effectively

Managing the weight of expectations requires a proactive and intentional approach. Here are some strategies to help individuals navigate this challenge:

1. Self-reflection: Take the time to reflect on personal values, goals, and aspirations. Understanding oneself and what truly matters can provide clarity and guide decision-making.

2. Open communication: Foster open and honest communication within the family and with key stakeholders. Discuss expectations, concerns, and aspirations to ensure everyone is on the same page.

3. Seek support: Surround yourself with a network of mentors, advisors, and peers who can provide guidance and support throughout the succession process. Their insights and experiences can be invaluable in managing expectations.

4. Set realistic goals: Establish realistic and achievable goals for the business and for personal growth. Breaking down larger

objectives into smaller, manageable steps can help alleviate the pressure and create a sense of progress.

5. Embrace flexibility: Recognize that plans may change and evolve over time. Embracing flexibility and adaptability can help individuals navigate unexpected challenges and adjust their expectations accordingly.

By acknowledging and addressing the weight of expectations, individuals involved in family business succession can better navigate the challenges and find fulfillment in their roles. It is important to remember that success is not solely defined by meeting external expectations, but by finding a balance between personal fulfillment, family legacy, and the long-term success of the business.

4.4 The Importance of Open Communication

Communication is the lifeblood of any successful relationship, and this holds true for family businesses as well. Open and honest communication is crucial during the succession planning process, as it helps to build trust, manage expectations, and ensure a smooth transition from one generation to the next.

4.4.1 Building Trust and Transparency

Trust is the foundation upon which successful family businesses are built. Without trust, conflicts can arise, and relationships can deteriorate. Open communication plays a vital role in building and maintaining trust within the family and the business.

By fostering an environment of transparency, family members can openly discuss their concerns, aspirations, and expectations. This transparency helps to align everyone's goals and ensures that decisions are made collectively, with the best interests of the business and the family at heart.

4.4.2 Managing Expectations

One of the biggest challenges in family business succession is managing the expectations of different family members. Each individual may have their own vision for the future of the business, and these visions may not always align.

Open communication allows family members to express their expectations and concerns openly. By facilitating these conversations, families can work together to find common ground and develop a shared vision for the future. This shared vision helps to minimize conflicts and ensures that everyone is working towards a common goal.

4.4.3 Resolving Conflict

Conflict is inevitable in any family business, especially during times of transition. However, open communication can help to address and resolve conflicts in a constructive manner.

By encouraging family members to express their concerns and grievances openly, conflicts can be brought to the surface and addressed proactively. This open dialogue allows for a deeper understanding of each other's perspectives and helps to find mutually beneficial solutions.

4.4.4 Facilitating Knowledge Transfer

Successful succession planning involves the transfer of knowledge and expertise from one generation to the next. Open communication is essential in facilitating this transfer of knowledge.

By encouraging open dialogue between generations, senior family members can share their wisdom, experiences, and insights with the next generation. This knowledge transfer ensures that the business's core values, traditions, and practices are preserved while allowing the next generation to bring fresh ideas and perspectives to the table.

4.4.5 Creating a Culture of Innovation

Open communication not only helps to preserve the legacy of the family business but also fosters a culture of innovation. By encouraging open dialogue and the sharing of ideas, family members can collaborate and explore new opportunities for growth and development.

This culture of innovation allows the family business to adapt to changing market conditions and stay ahead of the competition. It also empowers the next generation to take ownership of the business and contribute their unique skills and perspectives.

4.4.6 Seeking External Expertise

In some cases, open communication may involve seeking external expertise. Bringing in outside advisors, consultants, or mentors can provide an unbiased perspective and help facilitate difficult conversations.

These external experts can act as mediators, facilitators, or mentors, guiding the family through the succession planning process and ensuring that open communication is maintained. Their objective insights can help to overcome communication barriers and bridge the gap between different generations.

In conclusion, open communication is the key to successful family business succession. It builds trust, manages expectations, resolves conflicts, facilitates knowledge transfer, fosters innovation, and allows for the inclusion of external expertise. By prioritizing open communication, families can navigate the challenges of succession with greater ease and ensure the long-term success and sustainability of their businesses.

The Unseen Burden

The Legacy Conundrum

6.1 Preserving the Family Legacy

Preserving the family legacy is a crucial aspect of family business succession. It involves honoring the history, values, and traditions that have shaped the business while ensuring its relevance and sustainability in a rapidly changing world. This section explores the strategies and considerations involved in preserving the family legacy.

6.1.1 Understanding the Importance of Heritage

Before embarking on the journey of succession planning, it is essential to understand the significance of the family's heritage. The family legacy encompasses not only the tangible assets and achievements of the business but also the intangible aspects such as values, culture, and reputation. It is the foundation upon which the business has been built and the guiding force for future generations.

6.1.2 Documenting the Family History

One way to preserve the family legacy is by documenting the family history. This includes capturing the stories, experiences, and lessons learned from previous generations. By creating a comprehensive record of the family's journey, future generations can gain a deeper understanding of their roots and the values that have shaped the business.

6.1.3 Passing on Core Values and Traditions

Core values and traditions are the heart and soul of a family business. They provide a sense of identity and purpose, guiding decision-making and shaping the company's culture. Preserving the family legacy involves passing on these core values and traditions to the next generation. This can be done through formal training programs, mentorship, and leading by example.

6.1.4 Integrating Tradition with Innovation

Preserving the family legacy does not mean resisting change or innovation. It is essential to strike a balance between tradition and innovation to ensure the long-term success of the business. Embracing new technologies, exploring new markets, and adapting to evolving customer needs while staying true to the core values and traditions can help maintain the relevance and competitiveness of the family business.

6.1.5 Engaging the Next Generation

Engaging the next generation in the preservation of the family legacy is crucial for its continuity. By involving them in decision-making processes, encouraging their ideas and perspectives, and providing opportunities for growth and development, the family business can ensure a smooth transition while preserving the essence of the family legacy.

6.1.6 Building a Strong Succession Plan

A robust succession plan is essential for preserving the family legacy. It should outline the steps and strategies for transitioning leadership and ownership to the next generation while safeguarding the core values and traditions of the business. The plan should address issues such as leadership development, governance structures, and conflict resolution mechanisms to ensure a seamless transition and the preservation of the family legacy.

6.1.7 Communicating the Legacy to Stakeholders

Preserving the family legacy also involves effectively communicating it to stakeholders, including employees, customers, suppliers, and the wider community. Transparent and consistent communication about the family's values, traditions, and commitment to the business can foster trust, loyalty, and support from stakeholders, ensuring the continued success of the family business.

6.1.8 Seeking External Expertise

Preserving the family legacy can be a complex and challenging task. In some cases, seeking external expertise, such as consultants or advisors with experience in family business succession, can provide valuable insights and guidance. These professionals can help navigate the delicate balance between tradition and innovation, ensuring the preservation of the family legacy while driving the business forward.

Preserving the family legacy requires careful consideration, planning, and a commitment to honoring the past while embracing the future. By understanding the importance of heritage, documenting the family history, passing on core values and traditions, integrating tradition with innovation, engaging the next generation, building a strong succession plan, communicating the legacy to stakeholders, and seeking external expertise when needed, family businesses can successfully navigate the challenges of preserving their legacy while ensuring long-term success.

6.2 Embracing Change and Adaptation

Change is an inevitable part of life, and it is especially crucial in the context of family business succession. As the torch is passed from one generation to the next, the new leaders must be willing to embrace change and adapt to the evolving business landscape. This chapter explores the importance of embracing change, the benefits it brings, and strategies for successfully navigating the process.

6.2.1 The Need for Change

In today's fast-paced and dynamic business environment, change is not only necessary but also essential for survival. Family businesses that resist change risk becoming stagnant and losing their competitive edge. Embracing change allows businesses to stay relevant, seize new opportunities, and address emerging challenges. It is crucial for the next generation of leaders to recognize the need for change and understand its potential benefits.

6.2.2 Overcoming Resistance to Change

Change can be met with resistance, especially in family businesses where traditions and long-standing practices hold significant value. The resistance to change often stems from fear of the unknown, concerns about disrupting established relationships, and a desire to preserve the family legacy. However, it is essential to address and overcome this resistance to ensure the long-term success of the business.

One effective strategy for overcoming resistance to change is to foster open and transparent communication within the family and the business. By involving all stakeholders in the decision-making process and clearly articulating the reasons for change, leaders can help alleviate fears and build support for the necessary adaptations.

6.2.3 Embracing Innovation

Innovation is a key driver of growth and success in today's business landscape. Family businesses must be willing to embrace innovation and explore new ideas and technologies to remain competitive. This requires a mindset shift from "this is how we've always done it" to "how can we do it better?"

Encouraging a culture of innovation within the family business is crucial. This can be achieved by fostering an environment that values creativity, rewards risk-taking, and encourages continuous learning and improvement. Embracing innovation also involves seeking external perspectives and expertise, such as engaging with industry experts, consultants, and mentors who can provide fresh insights and ideas.

6.2.4 Adapting to Market Trends

Market trends and customer preferences are constantly evolving. Family businesses must be agile and adaptable to meet the changing needs of their target audience. This requires a deep understanding of market dynamics, staying informed about industry trends, and being willing to pivot when necessary.

Adapting to market trends involves conducting market research, analyzing customer feedback, and monitoring industry developments. By staying ahead of the curve, family businesses can proactively identify opportunities for growth and adjust their strategies accordingly.

6.2.5 Balancing Tradition and Innovation

While embracing change and adaptation is crucial, it is equally important to strike a balance between tradition and innovation. Family businesses often have a rich history and a strong sense of identity tied to their traditions and values. Preserving these traditions can provide a sense of continuity and stability, which is valued by both employees and customers.

However, it is essential to recognize that traditions alone may not be sufficient to sustain long-term success. Family businesses must be willing to evolve and adapt their practices to meet the demands of the modern business landscape. Striking the right balance between tradition and innovation requires thoughtful consideration, open dialogue, and a willingness to challenge the status quo when necessary.

In conclusion, embracing change and adaptation is a critical aspect of successful family business succession. It requires a willingness to recognize the need for change, overcome resistance, embrace innovation, adapt to market trends, and strike a balance between tradition and innovation. By doing so, family businesses can position themselves for long-term success and ensure a smooth transition to the next generation of leaders.

6.3 Finding the Right Balance

Finding the right balance between tradition and innovation is a critical aspect of navigating the challenges of family business succession. It requires careful consideration of the family's values, the business's core principles, and the evolving needs of the market. Striking this balance is not a one-size-fits-all approach; it requires a deep understanding of the unique dynamics and circumstances of each family business.

6.3.1 Embracing the Past while Embracing the Future

Preserving the family legacy is often a top priority for families transitioning their businesses to the next generation. The traditions, values, and history that have shaped the business are seen as a source of pride and identity. However, clinging too tightly to the past can hinder growth and innovation. It is essential to find a way to honor the past while embracing the future.

One way to achieve this balance is by identifying the core values and principles that have guided the family business throughout its history. These values can serve as a foundation for decision-making and provide a sense of continuity. At the same time, it is crucial to encourage and foster a culture of innovation and adaptability. This can be achieved by creating an environment that encourages new ideas, experimentation, and learning from both successes and failures.

6.3.2 Balancing Stability and Change

Maintaining stability while embracing change is another key aspect of finding the right balance in family business succession. Stability provides a sense of security and continuity, while change is necessary for growth and adaptation to a rapidly evolving business landscape.

To strike this balance, it is important to identify the areas where stability is crucial, such as core business processes, customer relationships, and the company's reputation. These areas should be preserved and protected to maintain the trust and loyalty of stakeholders. On the other hand, identifying areas where change is necessary, such as technology adoption, market expansion, and product innovation, is equally important. By carefully managing these areas of change, the family business can ensure its long-term viability and relevance.

6.3.3 Involving Multiple Perspectives

Finding the right balance in family business succession requires involving multiple perspectives and voices in the decision-making process. This includes not only family members but also key stakeholders, such as employees, customers, and advisors. Each perspective brings unique insights and experiences that can contribute to a more well-rounded and informed decision-making process.

Engaging in open and transparent communication is crucial to ensure that all perspectives are heard and considered. This can be achieved through regular family meetings, advisory boards, and structured feedback mechanisms. By actively seeking input from diverse sources, the family business can make more informed decisions that reflect the needs and aspirations of all stakeholders.

6.3.4 Adapting to Changing Market Dynamics

Finding the right balance in family business succession also requires a keen understanding of the changing dynamics of the market. The business landscape is constantly evolving, driven by technological advancements, shifting consumer preferences, and global economic trends. To remain competitive and relevant, family businesses must adapt and embrace change.

This adaptation can take various forms, such as investing in research and development, exploring new markets, or diversifying product offerings. It is essential to stay attuned to market trends, anticipate future challenges, and be willing to take calculated risks. By striking a balance between stability and change, family businesses can position themselves for long-term success in an ever-changing business environment.

In conclusion, finding the right balance between tradition and innovation is a crucial aspect of family business succession. It requires embracing the past while embracing the future, balancing stability and change, involving multiple perspectives, and adapting to changing market dynamics. By carefully navigating these complexities, family businesses can ensure a smooth transition and position themselves for long-term success.

6.4 Overcoming Resistance to Change

Change is often met with resistance, especially in the context of family business succession. The fear of the unknown, the attachment to tradition, and the reluctance to let go of control can all contribute to resistance. However, it is crucial to address and overcome this resistance in order to ensure a smooth and successful transition. Here are some strategies to help navigate and overcome resistance to change:

6.4.1 Understanding the Source of Resistance

Resistance to change can stem from various sources, and it is essential to identify and understand the underlying reasons. Some common sources of resistance in family business succession include:

1. Fear of losing control: The current generation may be hesitant to relinquish control and hand over the reins to the next generation. They may fear that their legacy will be compromised or that their influence will diminish.

2. Attachment to tradition: Family businesses often have deep-rooted traditions and values that have been passed down through generations. The resistance to change may arise from a desire to preserve these traditions and maintain the status quo.

3. Lack of trust: Resistance can also stem from a lack of trust between family members or between the current and next generations. Trust is crucial for successful succession, and

addressing any trust issues is essential for overcoming resistance.

4. Fear of failure: The fear of failure can be a significant barrier to change. The current generation may worry that the next generation will not be able to handle the responsibilities or make the right decisions, leading to the failure of the business.

6.4.2 Open and Transparent Communication

Open and transparent communication is key to overcoming resistance to change. It is important to create a safe and supportive environment where all family members can express their concerns, fears, and aspirations. Encourage open dialogue and active listening to ensure that everyone's voice is heard and respected.

By openly discussing the reasons for change and the potential benefits, you can help alleviate fears and address any misconceptions. Be transparent about the challenges and risks involved in the transition process, but also highlight the opportunities and positive outcomes that can arise from embracing change.

6.4.3 Building a Shared Vision

To overcome resistance, it is crucial to build a shared vision for the future of the family business. Involve all relevant stakeholders in the visioning process, including both the current and next generations. By collectively defining the goals, values, and direction of the business, you can create a sense of ownership and commitment among family members.

Ensure that the vision reflects a balance between preserving the family legacy and embracing innovation. Emphasize the importance of adapting to changing market dynamics and staying relevant in a competitive landscape while honoring the core values and traditions that have defined the family business.

6.4.4 Gradual and Incremental Change

Resistance to change can be mitigated by implementing gradual and incremental changes rather than sudden and drastic ones. This approach allows family members to adjust and adapt at their own pace, reducing the fear and uncertainty associated with rapid change.

Consider implementing pilot projects or small-scale initiatives to test new ideas and demonstrate their potential benefits. By showcasing the positive outcomes of these smaller changes, you can build confidence and trust among family members, making them more receptive to larger-scale changes in the future.

6.4.5 Leadership Development and Succession Planning

Effective leadership development and succession planning can help overcome resistance to change. By investing in the development of the next generation's leadership skills and capabilities, you can instill confidence and competence in their ability to lead the business forward.

Provide opportunities for the next generation to gain experience and exposure to different aspects of the business. Offer mentorship programs, training, and educational resources to support their growth and development. By demonstrating a commitment to their success, you can alleviate concerns and resistance to change.

6.4.6 Celebrating Success and Learning from Failure

Recognize and celebrate the successes that arise from embracing change. Highlight the positive outcomes and the benefits that have been realized as a result of the transition. By acknowledging and celebrating these achievements, you can reinforce the value of change and motivate family members to continue embracing it.

Additionally, it is important to learn from failures and setbacks along the way. Use these experiences as opportunities for growth and improvement. Encourage a culture of continuous learning and adaptation, where mistakes are seen as valuable lessons rather than reasons to resist change.

Overcoming resistance to change is a complex and ongoing process. It requires patience, empathy, and a commitment to open communication and collaboration. By understanding the sources of resistance, building a shared vision, implementing gradual changes, investing in leadership development, and celebrating successes, you can navigate the challenges of resistance and pave the way for a successful family business succession.

The Preparation Paradox

7.1 The Importance of Early Planning

Successful family business succession requires careful and strategic planning, and one of the key factors in this process is timing. Early planning allows for a thoughtful and deliberate approach to succession, giving the current and future generations ample time to prepare and adapt to their changing roles and responsibilities.

7.1.1 Setting the Foundation for Success

Early planning provides the opportunity to establish a solid foundation for the succession process. It allows the current generation to assess the strengths and weaknesses of the business, identify potential successors, and develop a clear vision for the future. By starting early, families can create a roadmap that outlines the steps and milestones necessary for a successful transition.

7.1.2 Identifying and Developing Next-Generation Leaders

One of the primary goals of early planning is to identify and develop the next generation of leaders within the family business. This involves assessing the skills, capabilities, and interests of potential successors and providing them with the necessary training and development opportunities to prepare them for their future roles. Early planning allows for a gradual and structured approach to leadership development, ensuring that the next generation is equipped with the knowledge and skills required to lead the business effectively.

7.1.3 Addressing Succession Challenges and Risks

Early planning also provides the opportunity to address potential challenges and risks associated with succession. By identifying and addressing these issues early on, families can mitigate the impact they may have on the transition process. This includes addressing conflicts among family members, managing expectations, and developing contingency plans for unexpected events or circumstances.

7.1.4 Engaging in Open and Transparent Communication

Early planning facilitates open and transparent communication among family members, which is crucial for a successful succession. It allows for honest discussions about the future of the business, individual aspirations, and concerns. By fostering a culture of open communication, families can ensure that everyone's voices are heard and that decisions are made collectively, leading to a smoother and more harmonious transition.

7.1.5 Building a Support Network

Early planning also provides the opportunity to build a support network for the current and future generations. This includes engaging external advisors, such as lawyers, accountants, and business consultants, who can provide guidance and expertise throughout the succession process. Additionally, families can establish mentorship programs or seek out peer networks to connect with other business families who have gone through similar transitions, allowing for shared experiences and learning.

7.1.6 Adapting to Changing Circumstances

Early planning allows families to adapt to changing circumstances and market conditions. By starting the planning process early, families have the flexibility to adjust their strategies and plans as needed, ensuring that the business remains resilient and competitive in an ever-evolving landscape. This adaptability is crucial for long-term success and sustainability.

In conclusion, early planning is essential for a successful family business succession. It provides the foundation for a smooth transition, allows for the identification and development of next-generation leaders, addresses potential challenges and risks, fosters open communication, builds a support network, and enables adaptability to changing circumstances. By recognizing the importance of early planning and taking proactive steps, families can navigate the complexities of succession with confidence and ensure the long-term success of their businesses.

7.2 Preparing the Next Generation

Preparing the next generation for leadership roles within the family business is a crucial step in ensuring a smooth and successful transition. It involves not only imparting the necessary skills and knowledge but also instilling the right mindset and values that align with the family's legacy and vision. This section explores the various aspects of preparing the next generation and provides practical strategies for effective succession planning.

7.2.1 Identifying Potential Leaders

The first step in preparing the next generation is identifying individuals within the family who have the potential to assume leadership roles. This process involves assessing their skills, strengths, and interests, as well as their commitment to the family business. It is essential to consider both their technical abilities and their leadership qualities, such as decision-making, communication, and problem-solving skills.

7.2.2 Providing Education and Training

Once potential leaders have been identified, it is crucial to provide them with the necessary education and training to develop their skills and knowledge. This can include formal education, such as business or management degrees, as well as specialized training programs tailored to the specific needs of the family business. Additionally, mentorship programs and internships can offer valuable hands-on experience and guidance from experienced family members or industry professionals.

7.2.3 Fostering a Growth Mindset

Preparing the next generation goes beyond technical skills and knowledge. It is equally important to foster a growth mindset that encourages continuous learning, adaptability, and innovation. This mindset enables future leaders to embrace change, take calculated risks, and seek new opportunities for the family business. Encouraging an entrepreneurial spirit and a willingness to challenge the status quo can help the next generation navigate the evolving business landscape.

7.2.4 Developing Emotional Intelligence

Emotional intelligence is a critical trait for effective leadership, particularly in a family business context. Developing emotional intelligence involves understanding and managing one's emotions and those of others. It includes skills such as empathy, self-awareness, and effective communication. By nurturing emotional intelligence in the next generation, family businesses can foster healthy relationships, resolve conflicts, and build trust among family members and employees.

7.2.5 Encouraging Collaboration and Teamwork

Preparing the next generation also involves fostering a collaborative and inclusive culture within the family business. This means encouraging teamwork, open communication, and the ability to work effectively with diverse individuals. By promoting collaboration, family businesses can leverage the collective strengths and perspectives of family members, creating a more resilient and innovative organization.

7.2.6 Balancing Family and Business Dynamics

One of the unique challenges of preparing the next generation in a family business is navigating the complex dynamics between family and business. It is essential to strike a balance between family relationships and professional responsibilities. This involves setting clear expectations, establishing boundaries, and promoting fairness and transparency in decision-making processes. By addressing these dynamics proactively, family businesses can minimize conflicts and ensure a harmonious transition of leadership.

7.2.7 Providing Opportunities for Leadership Development

To prepare the next generation for leadership roles, it is crucial to provide them with opportunities to develop their leadership skills and gain practical experience. This can include assigning them specific responsibilities within the business, allowing them to make decisions and learn from their successes and failures. Additionally, creating leadership development programs or initiatives can provide structured learning opportunities and mentorship from experienced family members or external advisors.

7.2.8 Nurturing a Sense of Ownership and Responsibility

Preparing the next generation involves nurturing a sense of ownership and responsibility for the family business. This can be achieved by involving them in strategic decision-making processes, encouraging them to contribute their ideas and perspectives, and gradually increasing their level of responsibility over time. By instilling a sense of ownership, family businesses can ensure the long-term commitment and dedication of the next generation.

In conclusion, preparing the next generation for leadership roles within the family business is a multifaceted process that requires careful planning and consideration. It involves identifying potential leaders, providing education and training, fostering a growth mindset, developing emotional intelligence, encouraging collaboration, balancing family and business dynamics, providing leadership development opportunities, and nurturing a sense of ownership and responsibility. By investing in the preparation of the next generation, family businesses can secure a successful and sustainable future.

7.3 Transitioning Leadership Responsibilities

Transitioning leadership responsibilities within a family business is a pivotal moment that requires careful consideration and planning. It involves passing the torch from one generation to the next, ensuring a smooth transfer of power and authority. However, this process is not without its challenges and complexities. In this section, we will explore the key factors to consider when transitioning leadership responsibilities and provide practical strategies for a successful handover.

7.3.1 Identifying the Right Successor

One of the most critical aspects of transitioning leadership responsibilities is identifying the right successor. This decision should not be taken lightly, as it will shape the future of the business. It is essential to evaluate potential candidates based on their skills, experience, and alignment with the family's values and vision. Consider their ability to lead, innovate, and adapt to changing market dynamics. Engage in open and honest discussions with family members and key stakeholders to gain different perspectives and insights.

7.3.2 Developing a Succession Plan

A well-defined succession plan is crucial for a smooth transition of leadership responsibilities. It outlines the steps and timeline for transferring power, ensuring clarity and transparency for all parties involved. The plan should include a detailed assessment of the current leadership's strengths and weaknesses, as well as the development needs of the successor. It should also address potential challenges and contingencies, such as unexpected events or emergencies. Regularly review and update the succession plan to adapt to evolving circumstances.

7.3.3 Communicating the Transition

Effective communication is paramount when transitioning leadership responsibilities. It is essential to involve all relevant stakeholders, including family members, employees, and external partners. Transparently communicate the reasons behind the transition, emphasizing the long-term vision and goals of the business. Address any concerns or uncertainties and provide opportunities for open dialogue and feedback. Clear and consistent communication builds trust and minimizes resistance during the transition process.

7.3.4 Mentoring and Knowledge Transfer

Successful leadership transition requires the transfer of knowledge and expertise from the outgoing leader to the successor. Establish a mentoring program that allows for the sharing of insights, experiences, and best practices. Encourage the outgoing leader to actively mentor and guide the successor, fostering a supportive and collaborative environment. This knowledge transfer ensures continuity and helps the successor navigate the challenges they may face in their new role.

7.3.5 Managing Resistance and Emotions

Transitioning leadership responsibilities can evoke a range of emotions, both for the outgoing leader and the successor. The outgoing leader may experience a sense of loss, while the successor may feel overwhelmed by the weight of expectations. It is crucial to acknowledge and address these emotions openly and empathetically. Provide support and resources, such as coaching or counseling, to help individuals navigate the emotional aspects of the transition. Encourage open dialogue and create a safe space for expressing concerns and fears.

7.3.6 Monitoring and Evaluation

Once the transition of leadership responsibilities is complete, it is essential to monitor and evaluate the progress of the successor. Regularly assess their performance and provide constructive feedback to support their growth and development. Establish key performance indicators (KPIs) to measure their effectiveness in leading the business. Continuously review and refine the succession plan as needed to ensure the ongoing success of the business.

Transitioning leadership responsibilities within a family business is a complex and multifaceted process. It requires careful planning, open communication, and a focus on developing the next generation of leaders. By identifying the right successor, developing a comprehensive succession plan, fostering mentorship and knowledge transfer, managing resistance and emotions, and monitoring and evaluating the successor's progress, family businesses can navigate this transition successfully and ensure the long-term sustainability and prosperity of the business.

7.4 Dealing with Unexpected Events

7.4.1 Embracing Flexibility and Adaptability

One of the key factors in successfully navigating unexpected events in family business succession is the ability to embrace flexibility and adaptability. Unexpected events can range from sudden health issues or accidents to economic downturns or industry disruptions. These events can significantly impact the succession plan and require quick thinking and adaptability to ensure the smooth continuation of the business.

To effectively deal with unexpected events, it is crucial to have a mindset that embraces change and is open to exploring alternative solutions. This requires a willingness to let go of rigid plans and adapt to the new circumstances. By being flexible, family business owners can better respond to unexpected events and make necessary adjustments to the succession plan.

7.4.2 Establishing Contingency Plans

To mitigate the impact of unexpected events, it is essential to establish contingency plans as part of the overall succession strategy. These plans should outline alternative courses of action that can be implemented in the event of unforeseen circumstances. Contingency plans may include identifying potential successors who can step in temporarily or permanently, establishing emergency funds to address financial challenges, or developing alternative business strategies to navigate industry disruptions.

By proactively developing contingency plans, family business owners can minimize the negative impact of unexpected events and ensure the continuity of the business. It is important to regularly review and update these plans to account for any changes in the business or external environment.

7.4.3 Seeking Professional Advice and Support

Dealing with unexpected events can be overwhelming, especially when they have a significant impact on the family business. In such situations, seeking professional advice and support can be invaluable. Experienced advisors, such as lawyers, accountants, and business consultants, can provide guidance and expertise in navigating unexpected events and their implications for the succession plan.

These professionals can help assess the situation, identify potential risks and opportunities, and provide recommendations on the best course of action. They can also assist in implementing contingency plans and ensuring compliance with legal and financial requirements. Additionally, seeking support from industry associations or networking with other family business owners who have faced similar challenges can provide valuable insights and perspectives.

7.4.4 Communicating Transparently and Effectively

During times of unexpected events, clear and transparent communication becomes even more critical. Family members, employees, and stakeholders need to be kept informed about the situation and any changes to the succession plan. Open communication helps build trust, reduces uncertainty, and fosters collaboration in finding solutions.

It is important to communicate not only the challenges but also the steps being taken to address them. This includes sharing updates on the contingency plans, seeking input and feedback from relevant parties, and providing reassurance about the long-term stability of the business. Effective communication can help alleviate anxiety and ensure that everyone is working together towards a common goal.

7.4.5 Maintaining Resilience and Emotional Well-being

Dealing with unexpected events can be emotionally challenging for family business owners. It is important to prioritize self-care and maintain resilience during these times. This includes seeking support from family, friends, or professional counselors to cope with the stress and emotional strain.

Taking breaks, practicing mindfulness or meditation, and engaging in activities outside of work can also help maintain emotional well-being. By prioritizing self-care, family business owners can better navigate the challenges of unexpected events and make sound decisions for the future of the business.

In conclusion, unexpected events are an inevitable part of life and can significantly impact the succession planning process in family businesses. By embracing flexibility, establishing contingency plans, seeking professional advice, communicating transparently, and maintaining emotional well-being, family business owners can effectively navigate these unexpected events and ensure the long-term success of their businesses.

Generational Chasm

8.1 Understanding Generational Differences

One of the key factors that can contribute to communication breakdowns within a family business is the presence of generational differences. Each generation brings its own unique set of values, beliefs, and communication styles, which can sometimes clash with those of other generations. Understanding and acknowledging these differences is crucial for effective communication and successful succession planning.

8.1.1 Values and Beliefs

Generational differences often stem from variations in values and beliefs that have been shaped by the social, economic, and cultural contexts in which each generation has grown up. For example, older generations may prioritize loyalty, tradition, and stability, while younger generations may value innovation, flexibility, and work-life balance. These differing values can lead to misunderstandings and conflicts if not properly addressed.

To bridge the gap, it is important to foster an environment of open dialogue and mutual respect. Encouraging family members from different generations to share their perspectives and actively listen to one another can help build understanding and empathy. Recognizing that there is no right or wrong set of values and beliefs can also promote a more inclusive and collaborative approach to decision-making.

8.1.2 Communication Styles

Another aspect of generational differences is the variation in communication styles. Older generations may prefer face-to-face conversations and formal written communication, while younger generations may rely more on digital platforms and informal modes of communication such as instant messaging and social media. These differences in communication preferences can lead to misinterpretations and misunderstandings if not effectively managed.

To bridge the communication gap, it is important to establish clear channels of communication that cater to the preferences of each generation. This may involve implementing a combination of traditional and digital communication methods to ensure that all family members feel comfortable and included. Regular family meetings, both in-person and virtual, can provide a platform for open and transparent communication, allowing each generation to express their thoughts and concerns.

8.1.3 Work Ethic and Expectations

Generational differences can also manifest in work ethic and expectations. Older generations may have a strong work ethic and place a high value on loyalty and dedication to the family business. On the other hand, younger generations may prioritize work-life balance and seek opportunities for personal growth and development outside of the business. These differing work ethics and expectations can create tension and conflicts if not properly addressed.

To bridge the gap, it is important to foster a culture of mutual understanding and flexibility. Recognizing and appreciating the contributions and perspectives of each generation can help create a sense of unity and shared purpose. Implementing flexible work arrangements and providing opportunities for professional development and growth can also help meet the expectations of younger generations while ensuring the continuity and success of the family business.

8.1.4 Bridging the Gap

Bridging the generational gap requires a proactive and inclusive approach. It involves creating an environment where all family members feel heard, valued, and respected. Here are some strategies to help bridge the communication divide:

1. Foster open and transparent communication: Encourage family members from different generations to share their thoughts, concerns, and ideas openly. Create a safe space for dialogue and actively listen to each other's perspectives.

2. Embrace technology: Incorporate digital communication tools and platforms that cater to the preferences of younger generations while ensuring that older generations feel comfortable and included. This can help bridge the gap between different communication styles.

3. Promote intergenerational collaboration: Encourage collaboration and teamwork

across generations. Assign cross-generational mentorship and partnership opportunities to foster knowledge sharing and mutual learning.

4. Seek professional guidance: Consider engaging the services of a professional facilitator or consultant who specializes in family business succession. They can provide objective insights and help navigate the challenges associated with generational differences.

By understanding and embracing generational differences, family businesses can create a harmonious and collaborative environment that supports effective communication and successful succession planning.

8.2 Bridging the Communication Gap

Effective communication is the cornerstone of any successful business, and family businesses are no exception. However, when multiple generations are involved, communication can become strained due to differences in values, perspectives, and communication styles. Bridging the communication gap is crucial for maintaining harmony, fostering collaboration, and ensuring a smooth transition of leadership and responsibilities.

8.2.1 Understanding Generational Differences

To bridge the communication gap, it is essential to first understand the generational differences that exist within the family business. Each generation brings its own set of values, beliefs, and communication preferences shaped by the historical and cultural context in which they grew up.

The older generation, often referred to as the "Traditionalists" or "Silent Generation," values loyalty, respect for authority, and a strong work ethic. They tend to prefer face-to-face communication and may be more reserved in expressing their opinions.

The Baby Boomers, born between 1946 and 1964, are known for their ambition, competitiveness, and desire for personal fulfillment. They value teamwork and collaboration and tend to prefer phone calls and in-person meetings for communication.

Generation X, born between 1965 and 1980, grew up during a time of rapid technological advancements. They are independent, adaptable, and value work-life balance. Gen Xers are comfortable with email and other digital communication methods.

Millennials, also known as Generation Y, were born between 1981 and 1996. They are tech-savvy, socially conscious, and value flexibility and work-life integration. Millennials prefer instant messaging, video calls, and other digital communication platforms.

Generation Z, born after 1997, is the first generation to grow up entirely in the digital age. They are highly connected, entrepreneurial, and value authenticity. Gen Zers prefer communication through social media, texting, and other digital platforms.

8.2.2 Building Trust and Collaboration

Building trust and fostering collaboration between different generations is crucial for effective communication within a family business. Trust is the foundation upon which open and honest communication can thrive. Here are some strategies to bridge the communication gap and build trust:

1. Active Listening: Encourage all generations to actively listen to one another without interruption or judgment. This creates an environment where everyone feels heard and valued.

2. Empathy and Understanding: Encourage each generation to understand and appreciate the perspectives and experiences of others. This helps to foster empathy and build bridges of understanding.

3. Clear and Transparent Communication: Establish clear channels of communication and encourage open and transparent dialogue. This includes regular family meetings, team-building exercises, and one-on-one conversations.

4. Respectful Conflict Resolution: Teach conflict resolution skills to all generations within the family business. Encourage respectful and constructive discussions to resolve conflicts and find common ground.

5. Mentorship and Reverse Mentorship: Facilitate mentorship programs where older generations can share their wisdom and

experience with younger generations. Similarly, encourage younger generations to mentor older generations in areas such as technology and digital communication.

8.2.3 Effective Communication Strategies

In addition to building trust and collaboration, implementing effective communication strategies can help bridge the gap between generations within a family business. Here are some strategies to consider:

1. Tailor Communication Styles: Recognize that different generations may have different communication preferences. Adapt your communication style to meet the needs of each generation, whether it's face-to-face meetings, phone calls, emails, or digital platforms.

2. Embrace Technology: Embrace technology and digital communication tools to facilitate communication between different generations. This can include using project management software, video conferencing platforms, and instant messaging apps.

3. Regular Communication Channels: Establish regular communication channels, such as weekly or monthly meetings, to keep all generations informed and engaged. This ensures that everyone is on the same page and reduces the likelihood of misunderstandings.

4. Document and Share Information: Document important information, decisions, and processes to ensure clarity and consistency. Share this information with all generations to promote transparency and avoid miscommunication.

5. Training and Development: Provide training and development opportunities for all generations to enhance their communication skills. This can include workshops on active listening, conflict resolution, and effective presentation skills.

By implementing these strategies, family businesses can bridge the communication gap between different generations, fostering understanding, collaboration, and a shared vision for the future. Effective communication is essential for a smooth transition of leadership and the long-term success of the family business.

8.3 Building Trust and Collaboration

Trust and collaboration are essential elements for the success of any family business, especially during the process of succession. Without trust, communication breaks down, conflicts arise, and decision-making becomes difficult. Collaboration, on the other hand, fosters a sense of unity and shared purpose, enabling family members to work together towards common goals. In this section, we will explore strategies for building trust and fostering collaboration within the family business.

8.3.1 Establishing Open and Transparent Communication

Open and transparent communication is the foundation for building trust within a family business. It is crucial to create an environment where family members feel comfortable expressing their thoughts, concerns, and aspirations. Encouraging open dialogue allows for the sharing of ideas, perspectives, and feedback, which can lead to better decision-making and problem-solving. Regular family meetings, both formal and informal, can provide a platform for open communication and help address any issues or conflicts that may arise.

8.3.2 Defining Roles and Responsibilities

Clearly defining roles and responsibilities is essential for effective collaboration within a family business. Each family member should have a defined role that aligns with their skills, interests, and aspirations. This clarity helps to avoid confusion, minimize conflicts, and ensure that everyone understands their contributions to the business. Regularly reviewing and updating these roles and responsibilities can also help accommodate changes in the business and the family dynamics.

8.3.3 Encouraging Shared Decision-Making

Involving family members in the decision-making process can foster a sense of ownership and collaboration. By seeking input from all relevant stakeholders, decisions can be made collectively, considering different perspectives and expertise. This approach not only strengthens trust but also promotes a culture of inclusivity and shared responsibility. It is important to establish clear decision-making processes and mechanisms to ensure that decisions are made in a fair and transparent manner.

8.3.4 Building a Culture of Accountability

Accountability is crucial for building trust and collaboration within a family business. Each family member should be accountable for their actions, commitments, and responsibilities. Establishing clear performance metrics, setting goals, and regularly reviewing progress can help ensure that everyone is working towards the same objectives. Holding family members accountable for their contributions and providing constructive feedback when necessary, can foster a culture of continuous improvement and mutual respect.

8.3.5 Resolving Conflicts Effectively

Conflicts are inevitable in any family business, but how they are resolved can either strengthen or weaken trust and collaboration. It is important to address conflicts promptly and constructively, focusing on finding mutually beneficial solutions rather than assigning blame. Mediation or the involvement of a neutral third party can be helpful in resolving complex or deeply rooted conflicts. By promoting open dialogue, active listening, and empathy, conflicts can be transformed into opportunities for growth and understanding.

8.3.6 Investing in Professional Development and Training

Investing in the professional development and training of family members can contribute to building trust and collaboration within the family business. Providing opportunities for skill-building, knowledge enhancement, and leadership development can empower family members to contribute effectively to the business. This investment demonstrates a commitment to their growth and success, fostering trust and collaboration by showing that their contributions are valued.

8.3.7 Celebrating Successes and Milestones

Celebrating successes and milestones is an important aspect of building trust and collaboration within a family business. Recognizing and acknowledging the achievements of family members fosters a positive and supportive environment. Regularly celebrating milestones, such as business anniversaries or significant achievements, can strengthen family bonds and create a sense of shared pride and accomplishment.

Building trust and collaboration within a family business is an ongoing process that requires continuous effort and commitment. By establishing open communication, defining roles and responsibilities, encouraging shared decision-making, promoting accountability, resolving conflicts effectively, investing in professional development, and celebrating successes, family businesses can navigate the challenges of succession with resilience and unity.

8.4 Effective Communication Strategies

Effective communication is the cornerstone of any successful business, and it becomes even more crucial during times of transition and change. In the context of family business succession, effective communication is essential for maintaining trust, resolving conflicts, and ensuring a smooth transition of leadership. Here, we will explore some key strategies that can help facilitate open and productive communication within the family business.

8.4.1 Establishing Open Lines of Communication

One of the first steps in fostering effective communication within a family business is to establish open lines of communication. This means creating an environment where all family members and stakeholders feel comfortable expressing their thoughts, concerns, and ideas. Encouraging regular and structured communication channels, such as family meetings or designated times for open discussions, can help ensure that everyone has a voice and feels heard.

8.4.2 Active Listening and Empathy

Effective communication is a two-way street, and active listening is a crucial component. Encourage family members to actively listen to one another, giving their full attention and seeking to understand the perspectives and emotions behind the words. Practicing empathy, putting oneself in the shoes of others, can also help foster understanding and build stronger relationships within the family business.

8.4.3 Clear and Transparent Communication

Clarity and transparency are vital in family business succession. Ambiguity and lack of information can lead to misunderstandings and conflicts. It is essential to communicate clearly and openly about the succession plan, including timelines, roles, and responsibilities. Providing regular updates and sharing information about the decision-making process can help build trust and alleviate anxieties.

8.4.4 Resolving Conflicts Constructively

Conflicts are inevitable in any business, and family businesses are no exception. However, conflicts within a family business can be particularly challenging due to the emotional dynamics involved. It is crucial to address conflicts promptly and constructively. Encourage family members to approach conflicts with a problem-solving mindset, focusing on finding mutually beneficial solutions rather than assigning blame. Mediation or involving a neutral third party can be helpful in resolving deep-rooted conflicts.

8.4.5 Embracing Technology for Communication

In today's digital age, technology offers numerous tools and platforms that can enhance communication within a family business. Utilizing email, video conferencing, project management software, and other collaborative tools can facilitate communication and ensure that everyone stays connected, regardless of their physical location. Embracing technology can also help bridge the generational gap by accommodating different communication preferences.

8.4.6 Regular Family Business Meetings

Family business meetings provide a structured platform for discussing important matters related to succession and the overall business. These meetings should be held regularly and involve all relevant family members and stakeholders. They offer an opportunity to review progress, address concerns, and make collective decisions. Setting an agenda and ensuring that all participants have an opportunity to contribute can help make these meetings productive and inclusive.

8.4.7 Seeking Professional Guidance

Sometimes, the complexities of family dynamics and succession planning require the expertise of professionals. Engaging the services of a family business consultant, mediator, or coach can provide valuable insights and guidance in navigating communication challenges. These professionals can help facilitate difficult conversations, offer objective perspectives, and provide strategies for effective communication.

8.4.8 Celebrating Successes and Milestones

Effective communication is not just about addressing challenges and conflicts; it is also about celebrating successes and milestones. Recognizing and acknowledging achievements within the family business can foster a positive and supportive environment. Regularly celebrating successes, whether big or small, can boost morale, strengthen relationships, and motivate family members to continue working towards shared goals.

In conclusion, effective communication is vital for navigating the communication breakdowns that often occur during family business succession. By establishing open lines of communication, practicing active listening and empathy, promoting clarity and transparency, resolving conflicts constructively, embracing technology, holding regular family business meetings, seeking professional guidance when needed, and celebrating successes, family businesses can foster understanding, collaboration, and ultimately, a successful transition of leadership.

Succession Stumbling Blocks

9.1 Lack of Succession Planning

Succession planning is the process of identifying and developing future leaders within a family business to ensure a smooth transition of power and responsibilities. Unfortunately, many family businesses neglect this crucial step, leading to significant challenges and potential disruptions in the succession process.

The Consequences of Neglecting Succession Planning

The lack of succession planning can have far-reaching consequences for both the business and the family. Without a clear plan in place, the transition of leadership can become chaotic and contentious, leading to conflicts, power struggles, and even the potential collapse of the business.

One of the primary consequences of neglecting succession planning is the uncertainty it creates. Without a designated successor or a clear roadmap for the transition, family members and employees may feel anxious and unsure about the future of the business. This uncertainty can lead to a loss of morale, decreased productivity, and a decline in the overall performance of the company.

Another consequence of the lack of succession planning is the potential for family conflicts to arise. When there is no clear plan in place, family members may have different expectations and aspirations for the future of the business. This can lead to disagreements, rivalries, and even estrangement among family members, which can have a detrimental impact on both the business and the family dynamics.

The Importance of Succession Planning

Succession planning is not just about ensuring a smooth transition of power; it is also about safeguarding the legacy and continuity of the family business. By proactively planning for the future, family businesses can mitigate risks, maintain stability, and preserve the values and traditions that have been built over generations.

One of the key benefits of succession planning is the ability to identify and develop future leaders within the family. By identifying potential successors early on, family businesses can provide them with the necessary training, mentorship, and opportunities to develop the skills and knowledge required to lead the business successfully. This not only ensures a seamless transition but also instills a sense of confidence and purpose in the next generation.

Succession planning also allows family businesses to address potential conflicts and challenges proactively. By engaging in open and honest discussions about the future of the business, family members can align their expectations, resolve conflicts, and establish a shared vision for the future. This collaborative approach fosters trust, strengthens family relationships, and sets the stage for a successful transition.

Overcoming the Lack of Succession Planning

If your family business has neglected succession planning, it is never too late to start. Here are some steps you can take to overcome this common stumbling block:

1. Start the conversation: Initiate open and honest discussions with family members about the importance of succession planning. Encourage everyone to share their thoughts, concerns, and aspirations for the future of the business.

2. Identify potential successors: Assess the skills, capabilities, and interests of family members who may be interested in taking on leadership roles in the future. Consider their qualifications, commitment, and alignment with the values and vision of the business.

3. Develop a succession plan: Work with family members, advisors, and professionals to create a comprehensive succession plan that outlines the timeline, roles, responsibilities, and development opportunities for potential successors. Ensure that the plan addresses both the strategic and emotional aspects of the transition.

4. Communicate the plan: Once the succession plan is in place, communicate it to all relevant stakeholders, including family members, employees, and key business partners. Be transparent about the process and the criteria for selecting the next leader.

5. Implement the plan: Execute the succession plan by providing the necessary training, mentorship, and support to potential successors. Monitor their progress, provide feedback, and adjust the plan as needed to ensure their readiness for leadership.

6. Seek external expertise: Consider engaging external advisors, consultants, or coaches who specialize in family business succession planning. Their expertise and impartial perspective can provide valuable insights and guidance throughout the process.

Remember, succession planning is an ongoing process that requires continuous evaluation and adjustment. By prioritizing succession planning and taking proactive steps to address the lack thereof, family businesses can navigate the challenges of generational transition with confidence and ensure the long-term success and sustainability of their legacy.

9.2 Sibling Rivalry and Family Conflicts

Sibling rivalry and family conflicts can be a significant stumbling block in the smooth transition of a family business from one generation to the next. These conflicts can arise due to a variety of factors, including differences in vision, power struggles, unresolved childhood issues, and unequal distribution of responsibilities and rewards. If not addressed effectively, these conflicts can not only disrupt the succession process but also have long-lasting negative effects on family relationships and the overall health of the business.

9.2.1 Understanding the Root Causes

To effectively address sibling rivalry and family conflicts, it is crucial to understand the root causes behind these issues. Sibling rivalry often stems from a deep-seated need for recognition, validation, and a desire to prove oneself. In a family business context, siblings may feel the need to compete for their parents' attention, approval, and ultimately, control of the business. These dynamics can be further exacerbated by unresolved childhood issues, such as favoritism, perceived inequalities, or unresolved conflicts between siblings.

Family conflicts, on the other hand, can arise from a lack of clear communication, differing expectations, and conflicting values and goals. As family members navigate the complexities of succession, their individual aspirations and visions for the business may clash, leading to disagreements and conflicts. Additionally, the unequal distribution of responsibilities and rewards can create resentment and animosity among siblings, further fueling conflicts.

9.2.2 Open and Transparent Communication

One of the most effective ways to address sibling rivalry and family conflicts is through open and transparent communication. Creating a safe and non-judgmental space for family members to express their thoughts, concerns, and aspirations can help foster understanding and empathy. Regular family meetings, facilitated by an impartial third party if necessary, can provide a platform for open dialogue and conflict resolution.

During these discussions, it is essential to encourage active listening and empathy. Each family member should have the opportunity to express their perspective and be heard without interruption or judgment. By actively listening to one another, family members can gain a deeper understanding of each other's motivations, fears, and aspirations, paving the way for finding common ground and resolving conflicts.

9.2.3 Establishing Clear Roles and Responsibilities

Another crucial step in mitigating sibling rivalry and family conflicts is to establish clear roles and responsibilities within the business. Ambiguity and lack of clarity regarding each sibling's role and authority can lead to power struggles and conflicts. By defining and communicating each individual's responsibilities, decision-making authority, and areas of expertise, you can minimize misunderstandings and reduce the potential for conflicts.

It is also important to ensure that the distribution of responsibilities and rewards is fair and equitable. Siblings should have a clear understanding of how their contributions to the business will be recognized and rewarded. This can help alleviate feelings of resentment and promote a sense of fairness and unity among family members.

9.2.4 Seeking Professional Mediation

In some cases, sibling rivalry and family conflicts may be deeply entrenched and difficult to resolve without external intervention. In such situations, seeking the assistance of a professional mediator or family business consultant can be invaluable. These professionals can provide an objective perspective, facilitate productive discussions, and help develop strategies for conflict resolution and improved communication.

Mediation can help family members navigate complex emotions, identify underlying issues, and work towards mutually beneficial solutions. The mediator can guide the family through a structured process that encourages open dialogue, active listening, and the development of practical solutions that address the root causes of conflicts.

9.2.5 Investing in Family Relationships

Lastly, it is crucial to recognize that family relationships are the foundation of a successful family business. Investing time and effort in nurturing these relationships can help prevent conflicts and foster a sense of unity and collaboration among siblings. Regular family activities, such as vacations, celebrations, and shared hobbies, can provide opportunities for family members to bond and strengthen their relationships outside of the business context.

Additionally, creating a family constitution or a set of guiding principles can help establish a shared vision, values, and goals for the family and the business. This document can serve as a reference point during times of conflict, reminding family members of their shared purpose and the importance of maintaining strong family relationships.

In conclusion, sibling rivalry and family conflicts can pose significant challenges during the succession process of a family business. However, by understanding the root causes, fostering open communication, establishing clear roles and responsibilities, seeking professional mediation when necessary, and investing in family relationships, it is possible to navigate these challenges and build a strong foundation for a successful and harmonious transition.

9.3 Resistance to Change

Change is often met with resistance, and this is especially true in the context of family business succession. When a new generation takes the reins, there is a natural inclination to maintain the status quo and resist any changes that may disrupt the familiar dynamics and traditions of the business. This resistance can come from both the outgoing generation, who may struggle to let go of their role and authority, as well as from the incoming generation, who may face resistance from family members and employees who are resistant to their new ideas and leadership style.

9.3.1 Understanding the Fear of the Unknown

Resistance to change often stems from a fear of the unknown. The outgoing generation may fear losing control and influence over the business they have built, while the incoming generation may fear making mistakes or not living up to the expectations placed upon them. Additionally, employees and other stakeholders may fear the potential disruption and uncertainty that comes with change. It is important to acknowledge and address these fears in order to effectively manage resistance to change.

9.3.2 Overcoming the Status Quo Bias

Humans have a natural tendency to prefer the status quo, even when it may not be in their best interest. This bias can be particularly strong in family businesses, where traditions and established ways of doing things hold significant value. Overcoming the status quo bias requires a willingness to challenge long-held beliefs and practices, and to embrace new ideas and approaches. It is important to create a culture that encourages innovation and continuous improvement, and to communicate the benefits of change to all stakeholders.

9.3.3 Communicating the Vision for Change

Resistance to change can often be mitigated through effective communication. It is crucial for the incoming generation to clearly articulate their vision for the future of the business and to communicate the reasons behind the proposed changes. By involving all stakeholders in the decision-making process and addressing their concerns and questions, the incoming generation can build trust and support for their vision. Regular and transparent communication is key to managing resistance and ensuring a smooth transition.

9.3.4 Building a Culture of Adaptability

To overcome resistance to change, it is important to foster a culture of adaptability within the family business. This involves creating an environment where experimentation and learning from failure are encouraged, and where employees feel empowered to contribute their ideas and perspectives. By embracing a growth mindset and valuing continuous learning and improvement, the business can better navigate the challenges of change and adapt to new market conditions and opportunities.

9.3.5 Addressing Emotional Attachments

Resistance to change in family businesses can often be rooted in emotional attachments to the business and its traditions. The outgoing generation may have a deep emotional connection to the business they have built and may struggle to let go and embrace change. It is important to acknowledge and address these emotional attachments, and to provide support and guidance to the outgoing generation as they navigate the transition. This may involve facilitating open and honest conversations about the emotional aspects of succession, and providing resources such as counseling or coaching to help individuals cope with the emotional challenges they may face.

9.3.6 Leading by Example

Leadership plays a crucial role in managing resistance to change. The incoming generation must lead by example and demonstrate their commitment to change through their actions. This involves being open to feedback, actively seeking input from others, and being willing to adapt and modify their plans based on new information. By modeling the behavior, they expect from others, the incoming generation can inspire confidence and trust, and encourage others to embrace change.

9.3.7 Celebrating Successes and Learning from Failures

Change can be a difficult and challenging process, but it is important to celebrate successes along the way. By acknowledging and rewarding progress, the incoming generation can motivate and inspire others to continue embracing change. It is also important to learn from failures and setbacks, and to use them as opportunities for growth and improvement. By adopting a mindset of continuous learning and improvement, the family business can navigate the challenges of change more effectively.

In conclusion, resistance to change is a common stumbling block in family business succession. By understanding the fear of the unknown, overcoming the status quo bias, communicating the vision for change, building a culture of adaptability, addressing emotional attachments, leading by example, and celebrating successes and learning from failures, the incoming generation can effectively manage resistance to change and ensure a successful transition. Embracing change is essential for the long-term success and sustainability of the family business, and by navigating resistance to change, the family can chart a course for a lasting legacy.

9.4 Lack of Leadership Development

One of the key factors that can hinder a successful transition in a family business is the lack of leadership development. Many family businesses struggle with identifying and nurturing the next generation of leaders within the family. This can lead to a leadership vacuum, causing instability and uncertainty in the business.

9.4.1 Identifying Potential Leaders

The first step in addressing the lack of leadership development is to identify potential leaders within the family. This involves assessing the skills, capabilities, and interests of family members who have the potential to take on leadership roles in the business. It is important to look beyond the obvious choices and consider individuals who may have different strengths and perspectives that can contribute to the future success of the business.

9.4.2 Providing Training and Development Opportunities

Once potential leaders have been identified, it is crucial to provide them with the necessary training and development opportunities to enhance their leadership skills. This can include formal education programs, mentorship initiatives, and on-the-job training. By investing in the development of future leaders, family businesses can ensure a smooth transition and continuity in leadership.

9.4.3 Encouraging Continuous Learning

Leadership development should not be seen as a one-time event but rather as an ongoing process. Encouraging continuous learning and personal growth among potential leaders is essential for their long-term success. This can be achieved through participation in industry conferences, networking events, and executive education programs. By staying updated on industry trends and best practices, potential leaders can bring fresh ideas and innovation to the business.

9.4.4 Fostering a Culture of Leadership

Creating a culture that values and promotes leadership is crucial for the development of future leaders. This involves instilling a sense of responsibility, accountability, and initiative among family members. By fostering a culture that encourages leadership at all levels of the organization, family businesses can ensure a pipeline of capable leaders who are ready to take on greater responsibilities when the time comes.

9.4.5 Succession Planning and Mentoring

Succession planning and mentoring play a vital role in leadership development. Family businesses should have a well-defined succession plan in place that outlines the process of transitioning leadership roles from one generation to the next. Mentoring programs can also be established to provide guidance and support to potential leaders, allowing them to learn from the experiences and wisdom of current leaders.

9.4.6 Embracing External Expertise

In some cases, family businesses may benefit from seeking external expertise to supplement the leadership development efforts within the family. This can involve hiring consultants or executive coaches who specialize in family business succession. These external experts can provide valuable insights, guidance, and support to both current and potential leaders, helping them navigate the complexities of succession.

9.4.7 Evaluating and Adjusting Leadership Development Strategies

Leadership development strategies should be regularly evaluated and adjusted to ensure their effectiveness. This involves gathering feedback from current and potential leaders, as well as other stakeholders in the business. By continuously assessing and refining leadership development initiatives, family businesses can adapt to changing circumstances and ensure that their leadership pipeline remains strong.

In conclusion, the lack of leadership development can pose significant challenges to family business succession. However, by identifying potential leaders, providing training and development opportunities, fostering a culture of leadership, and embracing external expertise, family businesses can overcome this stumbling block and ensure a smooth transition of leadership. Continuous learning, succession planning, and mentoring are also crucial components of effective leadership development strategies. By investing in the development of future leaders, family businesses can secure their long-term success and create a lasting legacy.

The Professional Pivot

10.1 Pros and Cons of Hiring External Leaders

When it comes to choosing the next leader for a family business, one of the key decisions is whether to hire an external candidate or promote someone from within the family or existing team. Both options have their advantages and disadvantages, and it is important to carefully evaluate them in the context of the specific business and family dynamics. In this section, we will explore the pros and cons of hiring external leaders.

10.1.1 Pros of Hiring External Leaders

Fresh Perspective and Expertise

One of the primary advantages of hiring an external leader is the fresh perspective and expertise they bring to the table. They can offer new ideas, strategies, and industry insights that may not have been considered within the family or existing team. Their experience in different organizations can bring valuable knowledge and best practices that can drive innovation and growth.

Objectivity and Impartiality

External leaders often have the advantage of being impartial and objective in their decision-making. They are not influenced by family dynamics or personal relationships, allowing them to make tough decisions solely based on what is best for the business. This objectivity can help avoid favoritism and ensure that decisions are made in the best interest of the company's long-term success.

Professional Network and Industry Connections

An external leader typically brings with them a professional network and industry connections that can be beneficial for the business. These connections can open doors to new partnerships, collaborations, and opportunities that may not have been accessible otherwise. Leveraging their network can help the business expand its reach and tap into new markets or customer segments.

Leadership and Management Skills

External leaders often have a proven track record of leadership and management skills. They have experience in leading teams, driving organizational change, and implementing effective strategies. Their expertise in managing complex business operations can bring stability and efficiency to the family business, ensuring its continued growth and success.

10.1.2 Cons of Hiring External Leaders

Lack of Familiarity with the Business and Family Dynamics

One of the main challenges of hiring an external leader is their lack of familiarity with the business and family dynamics. They may take time to understand the unique culture, values, and history of the family business, which can impact their ability to make informed decisions. Building trust and rapport with family members and existing employees may also take time and effort.

Bringing in an external leader can sometimes be met with resistance from family members and employees who may feel threatened or excluded from the decision-making process. This resistance can create tension and hinder the leader's ability to implement changes or gain support from key stakeholders. Managing these dynamics and fostering open communication is crucial to ensure a smooth transition.

Cultural Fit and Alignment with Family Values

Family businesses often have a strong emphasis on their unique culture and values. Hiring an external leader who does not align with these values can create a disconnect and lead to conflicts. It is essential to carefully assess the cultural fit and ensure that the leader shares the same vision and values as the family and the business.

Potential Disruption to Existing Team Dynamics

Introducing an external leader can disrupt existing team dynamics, especially if there are internal candidates who were expecting to be promoted. This can lead to resentment and a decline in morale among the team members. It is important to manage these dynamics proactively and provide support to the existing team during the transition.

In conclusion, hiring an external leader for a family business can bring fresh perspectives, expertise, and industry connections. They can provide objectivity and impartiality in decision-making and bring valuable leadership and management skills. However, it is crucial to consider the potential challenges such as lack of familiarity with the business and family dynamics, resistance from family members and employees, cultural fit, and disruption to existing team dynamics. Ultimately, the decision should be based on a thorough evaluation of the specific needs and goals of the family business, taking into account the long-term vision and sustainability of the organization.

10.2 Developing Internal Talent

One of the key decisions that family business owners face when planning for succession is whether to hire external leaders or nurture internal talent. While both options have their merits, developing internal talent can offer unique advantages and opportunities for the long-term success and sustainability of the business.

10.2.1 The Benefits of Developing Internal Talent

Developing internal talent allows the business to leverage the knowledge, experience, and commitment of individuals who are already familiar with the company's culture, values, and operations. By investing in the development of existing employees, the business can ensure a smooth transition of leadership while maintaining continuity and preserving the family's legacy.

1. **Cultural Continuity**: Internal talent development ensures that the family's values, traditions, and culture are passed down to the next generation. Employees who have grown

up within the business are more likely to understand and embody these values, creating a sense of continuity and preserving the unique identity of the family business.

2. **Knowledge and Expertise**: Employees who have been with the company for an extended period possess valuable institutional knowledge and industry-specific expertise. By developing these individuals, the business can tap into their deep understanding of the organization's history, operations, and customer base, which can be crucial for maintaining stability and driving future growth.

3. **Motivation and Loyalty**: Investing in the development of internal talent demonstrates a commitment to the growth and advancement of employees. This can foster a sense of loyalty and motivation among individuals who see a clear path for career progression within the organization. Employees who feel valued and supported are more likely to be engaged, dedicated, and committed to the long-term success of the business.

4. **Cost-Effectiveness**: Developing internal talent can be a cost-effective strategy compared to hiring external leaders. The expenses associated with recruitment, onboarding, and assimilation of new leaders can be significant. By investing in the development of existing employees, the business can save on these costs while also

benefiting from the familiarity and existing relationships that internal candidates bring to the table.

10.2.2 Strategies for Developing Internal Talent

To effectively develop internal talent, family businesses need to implement strategies that focus on identifying and nurturing high-potential individuals within the organization. Here are some key strategies to consider:

1. **Identifying Potential**: Implement a systematic process for identifying employees with the potential to assume leadership roles in the future. This can involve assessing their skills, competencies, and performance, as well as their alignment with the family's values and vision. Regular performance evaluations, feedback sessions, and talent assessments can help identify individuals who exhibit the qualities necessary for leadership positions.

2. **Providing Training and Development Opportunities**: Offer targeted training and development programs to enhance the skills and capabilities of identified high-potential employees. This can include leadership development workshops, mentoring programs, executive education courses, and cross-functional assignments. Providing opportunities for personal and professional growth not only prepares individuals for future leadership roles but also demonstrates the organization's commitment to their development.

3. **Creating a Succession Plan**: Develop a comprehensive succession plan that outlines the steps and timeline for transitioning key leadership positions to internal candidates. This plan should include clear criteria for advancement, a roadmap for development, and a process for evaluating and selecting potential successors. Regularly review and update the succession plan to ensure its alignment with the evolving needs of the business.

4. **Mentoring and Coaching**: Establish mentoring and coaching programs that pair high-potential employees with experienced leaders within the organization. This allows for the transfer of knowledge, skills, and insights from seasoned leaders to the next generation. Mentoring and coaching relationships can provide valuable guidance, support, and perspective to emerging leaders, helping them navigate the challenges of leadership and develop their own unique leadership style.

5. **Encouraging Continuous Learning**: Foster a culture of continuous learning and growth within the organization. Encourage employees to pursue ongoing education, attend industry conferences, and participate in professional development activities. Providing opportunities for learning and growth not only enhances the skills and knowledge of individuals but also contributes to the overall intellectual capital of the organization.

10.2.3 Balancing Internal and External Leadership

While developing internal talent is crucial for the long-term success of a family business, it is important to strike a balance between internal and external leadership. In some cases, hiring external leaders can bring fresh perspectives, new ideas, and specialized expertise that may be lacking within the organization. It is essential to evaluate the specific needs of the business and consider the potential benefits of both internal and external candidates when making leadership decisions.

By developing internal talent, family businesses can create a pipeline of capable leaders who are deeply invested in the success of the organization. This approach not only ensures a smooth transition of leadership but also preserves the family's legacy, values, and culture. However, it is important to recognize that developing internal talent requires a long-term commitment, strategic planning, and ongoing investment in the growth and development of employees.

In the next chapter, we will explore the emotional resilience required during farewells and the importance of supporting retiring family members as they navigate the transition from business to retirement.

10.3 Creating a Leadership Development Program

A leadership development program is a structured approach to identifying, nurturing, and preparing future leaders within the family business. It involves a systematic process of assessing leadership potential, providing targeted training and development opportunities, and creating a supportive environment for growth and learning. By investing in the development of internal talent, family businesses can cultivate a pipeline of capable leaders who understand the values, culture, and unique challenges of the organization.

10.3.1 Assessing Leadership Potential

Before embarking on the creation of a leadership development program, it is essential to identify individuals within the family who have the potential to assume leadership roles in the future. This assessment should go beyond traditional measures of competence and experience and consider factors such as passion, adaptability, and alignment with the family's values and vision.

One effective approach is to conduct a comprehensive talent review, which involves evaluating family members based on their skills, knowledge, and potential for growth. This process can include interviews, performance evaluations, and assessments to gain a holistic understanding of each individual's strengths and areas for development.

10.3.2 Designing a Development Curriculum

Once potential leaders have been identified, the next step is to design a development curriculum that addresses their specific needs and prepares them for future leadership roles. This curriculum should encompass a range of learning experiences, including formal training programs, mentoring relationships, job rotations, and exposure to different aspects of the business.

Formal training programs can include courses on leadership, strategic thinking, financial management, and other relevant topics. These programs can be conducted internally or externally, depending on the resources and expertise available within the family business.

Mentoring relationships play a crucial role in leadership development, as they provide aspiring leaders with guidance, support, and opportunities for learning from experienced family members or external mentors. These relationships can help individuals navigate the complexities of the family business and gain valuable insights from those who have successfully transitioned into leadership roles.

Job rotations allow potential leaders to gain exposure to different functional areas of the business, enabling them to develop a broad understanding of the organization and its operations. This hands-on experience helps individuals build a diverse skill set and prepares them for the challenges they may face as future leaders.

10.3.3 Creating a Supportive Environment

A leadership development program is most effective when it is supported by a culture that values learning, growth, and continuous improvement. Creating such an environment requires a commitment from the family business to provide the necessary resources, support, and opportunities for development.

One way to foster a supportive environment is by establishing a leadership development committee or task force, comprising family members, senior executives, and external advisors. This committee can oversee the implementation of the program, provide guidance and mentorship to aspiring leaders, and ensure that the development efforts align with the strategic goals of the business.

Additionally, it is essential to create a culture that encourages open communication, collaboration, and constructive feedback. This allows potential leaders to learn from their experiences, seek guidance when needed, and continuously improve their skills and capabilities.

10.3.4 Measuring Success and Adjusting the Program

To ensure the effectiveness of the leadership development program, it is crucial to establish clear metrics and regularly evaluate its impact. This can be done through performance evaluations, feedback from mentors and supervisors, and tracking the progress of individuals who have completed the program.

Based on the evaluation results, adjustments can be made to the program to address any gaps or areas for improvement. This iterative process allows the family business to refine its approach to leadership development and ensure that it remains relevant and aligned with the evolving needs of the organization.

By creating a leadership development program, family businesses can proactively prepare the next generation of leaders, ensuring a smooth transition and the long-term success of the business. This investment in internal talent not only strengthens the family's legacy but also fosters a sense of ownership, commitment, and continuity within the organization.

10.4 Finding the Right Leadership Fit

One of the most crucial decisions in the succession process is determining who will lead the family business in the next generation. This decision carries significant weight as it will shape the future direction and success of the company. Finding the right leadership fit involves a careful evaluation of both internal and external candidates, considering their skills, experience, values, and alignment with the family's vision.

10.4.1 Assessing Internal Candidates

When considering internal candidates, it is essential to evaluate their qualifications, capabilities, and potential for growth. Look for individuals who have demonstrated a strong work ethic, a passion for the business, and a willingness to learn and adapt. Assess their leadership skills, ability to make tough decisions, and their capacity to inspire and motivate others.

It is also crucial to consider the candidate's alignment with the family's values and long-term goals. A shared vision and commitment to the family's legacy can contribute to a smoother transition and ensure the preservation of the company's culture.

10.4.2 Developing Leadership Skills

If internal candidates lack certain leadership skills or experience, it is important to provide them with the necessary development opportunities. This can include mentorship programs, executive education, and leadership training. By investing in their growth and development, you can groom potential leaders and equip them with the skills needed to succeed in their new roles.

10.4.3 Hiring External Leaders

In some cases, the family may decide to bring in external leaders to lead the business. Hiring external leaders can bring fresh perspectives, new ideas, and specialized expertise to the organization. They can introduce innovative strategies and help the company adapt to changing market dynamics.

When considering external candidates, it is crucial to conduct a thorough evaluation of their qualifications, track record, and cultural fit. Look for individuals who have experience in the industry, a proven track record of success, and the ability to work collaboratively with the family and existing team members.

10.4.4 Balancing Internal and External Leadership

Finding the right leadership fit often involves striking a balance between internal and external candidates. It is not uncommon for family businesses to adopt a hybrid approach, where internal leaders are supported by external advisors or consultants. This allows for a combination of industry expertise, fresh perspectives, and the preservation of family values and culture.

The decision to hire external leaders or nurture internal talent should be based on a careful assessment of the business's needs, the capabilities of internal candidates, and the availability of suitable external candidates. It is important to consider the long-term implications of this decision and how it aligns with the family's vision for the future.

10.4.5 The Role of Succession Planning

Effective succession planning plays a crucial role in finding the right leadership fit. By identifying potential successors early on, the family can provide them with the necessary development opportunities and prepare them for future leadership roles. Succession planning also allows for a smooth transition and minimizes disruptions to the business.

It is important to involve key stakeholders, including family members, board members, and trusted advisors, in the succession planning process. Their input and perspectives can help ensure that the decision regarding the leadership fit is well-informed and aligned with the overall goals of the business.

10.4.6 Continuous Evaluation and Adaptation

Finding the right leadership fit is not a one-time decision but an ongoing process. As the business evolves and market conditions change, it is important to continuously evaluate the performance and effectiveness of the chosen leaders. Regular feedback, performance reviews, and open communication channels can help identify areas for improvement and ensure that the leadership fit remains aligned with the business's needs.

In conclusion, finding the right leadership fit is a critical aspect of family business succession. It requires a careful evaluation of internal and external candidates, considering their qualifications, skills, values, and alignment with the family's vision. By investing in the development of internal candidates and conducting thorough assessments of external candidates, family businesses can ensure a smooth transition and set the stage for long-term success.

The Long Goodbye

11.1 Preparing for Retirement

Retirement is a significant milestone in anyone's life, but for family business owners, it can be an especially complex and emotional process. After dedicating years, if not decades, to building and nurturing a successful business, the prospect of stepping away can evoke a range of emotions, from excitement and relief to anxiety and loss. In this section, we will explore the various aspects of preparing for retirement and offer guidance on how to navigate this transition with emotional resilience.

11.1.1 Shifting Mindset

One of the first steps in preparing for retirement is shifting your mindset from being actively involved in the day-to-day operations of the business to a more advisory or passive role. This shift can be challenging, as it requires letting go of control and trusting the next generation or external leaders to take the reins. It is essential to recognize that retirement does not mean the end of your involvement in the business but rather a new phase where your role evolves. Embracing this mindset shift can help alleviate some of the emotional strain associated with retirement.

11.1.2 Creating a Succession Plan

A well-thought-out succession plan is crucial for a smooth transition into retirement. This plan should outline the steps and timeline for transferring leadership and ownership responsibilities to the next generation or external leaders. By involving key stakeholders, such as family members and trusted advisors, in the succession planning process, you can ensure that everyone's expectations and concerns are addressed. This collaborative approach can also help alleviate any anxiety or uncertainty surrounding retirement.

11.1.3 Identifying Personal Goals and Interests

Retirement provides an opportunity to explore new interests and passions outside of the business. It is essential to take the time to reflect on your personal goals and aspirations for this next phase of life. Consider what activities or hobbies bring you joy and fulfillment and how you can incorporate them into your retirement plan. By identifying and pursuing your personal interests, you can find a sense of purpose and fulfillment beyond the business.

11.1.4 Building a Support Network

Retirement can be an emotionally challenging time, as it often involves a significant shift in identity and routine. Building a support network of family, friends, and fellow business owners who have gone through a similar transition can provide invaluable emotional support and guidance. Surrounding yourself with individuals who understand the unique challenges of retiring from a family business can help you navigate the emotional ups and downs with resilience.

11.1.5 Seeking Professional Guidance

Retirement planning is a complex process that requires careful consideration of financial, legal, and tax implications. Seeking professional guidance from financial advisors, estate planners, and tax experts can help ensure that your retirement plan is comprehensive and aligned with your long-term goals. These professionals can provide valuable insights and strategies to maximize your financial security and minimize potential risks during the retirement transition.

11.1.6 Embracing New Roles and Opportunities

Retirement from the family business does not mean the end of your professional life. Many retired business owners find fulfillment in mentoring the next generation, serving on advisory boards, or pursuing philanthropic endeavors. Embracing these new roles and opportunities can provide a sense of purpose and continued engagement in the business world while allowing you to step back from the day-to-day responsibilities.

8.1.7 Taking Care of Emotional Well-being

Retirement can bring a mix of emotions, including a sense of loss, identity crisis, and uncertainty about the future. It is crucial to prioritize your emotional well-being during this transition. Engaging in activities that promote self-care, such as exercise, meditation, or therapy, can help manage stress and anxiety. Additionally, maintaining open lines of communication with loved ones and seeking support when needed can contribute to a smoother emotional transition into retirement.

Preparing for retirement as a family business owner requires careful planning, emotional resilience, and a willingness to embrace change. By shifting your mindset, creating a succession plan, identifying personal goals, building a support network, seeking professional guidance, embracing new roles, and prioritizing emotional well-being, you can navigate this transition with grace and set the stage for a fulfilling retirement beyond the business.

11.2 Coping with Loss of Identity

Retirement marks a significant milestone in the life of a family business owner. It is a time of transition, where the torch is passed on to the next generation, and the retiree steps away from the business they have dedicated their life to. However, this transition can also bring about a profound sense of loss and a struggle with identity for the retiring owner.

11.2.1 The Emotional Impact

For many family business owners, their identity is deeply intertwined with their role in the business. They have spent years building and nurturing their company, and it has become a significant part of who they are. As they retire and hand over the reins to the next generation, they may experience a sense of loss and a questioning of their purpose and value outside of the business.

The emotional impact of this loss of identity can be profound. Retiring owners may feel a sense of emptiness, a loss of purpose, and a lack of direction. They may struggle with feelings of self-doubt and wonder if they are still relevant and valuable without their business. It is essential to acknowledge and address these emotions to ensure a smooth transition and emotional well-being for the retiring owner.

11.2.2 Rediscovering Identity

Coping with the loss of identity requires a process of rediscovery and self-reflection. Retiring family business owners need to explore who they are beyond their role in the business and find new sources of meaning and purpose in their lives. This can be a challenging and transformative journey, but it is essential for their emotional well-being and overall happiness.

One way to begin this process is by engaging in activities and hobbies that bring joy and fulfillment. Retiring owners can explore new interests, pursue lifelong passions, or even embark on new ventures outside of the business world. This allows them to discover new aspects of themselves and find a sense of purpose beyond their previous role.

Additionally, seeking support from loved ones, friends, and professional counselors can be invaluable during this transition. Having a strong support system can provide emotional guidance, encouragement, and a safe space to express feelings of loss and uncertainty. It is crucial for retiring owners to surround themselves with individuals who understand and empathize with their experience.

11.2.3 Embracing Personal Growth

Retirement presents an opportunity for personal growth and self-improvement. Retiring family business owners can use this time to invest in their own development and explore new avenues of learning. They can pursue educational opportunities, attend workshops or seminars, or even consider volunteering or mentoring others in their field of expertise.

By embracing personal growth, retiring owners can expand their horizons, gain new skills, and find fulfillment in continuous learning. This not only helps them build a new sense of identity but also allows them to contribute their knowledge and experience to the broader community.

11.2.4 Seeking Purpose Beyond Business

Finding purpose beyond the business is a crucial aspect of coping with the loss of identity. Retiring family business owners can explore ways to make a positive impact in their communities or engage in philanthropic endeavors. By aligning their values and passions with meaningful causes, they can find a new sense of purpose and fulfillment.

Additionally, retiring owners can consider mentoring and supporting the next generation of entrepreneurs. Sharing their wisdom and experiences can be incredibly rewarding and provide a sense of purpose as they contribute to the success of others. This not only helps them maintain a connection to the business world but also allows them to leave a lasting legacy.

In conclusion, coping with the loss of identity is a significant challenge for retiring family business owners. However, by acknowledging and addressing these emotions, engaging in self-reflection, embracing personal growth, and seeking purpose beyond the business, they can navigate this transition with resilience and find fulfillment in the next chapter of their lives.

11.3 Supporting Emotional Well-being

Emotional well-being is a crucial aspect of the transition process for outgoing leaders in a family business. After dedicating their lives to building and growing the business, stepping away can be an emotionally challenging experience. It is essential to provide support and resources to help them navigate this significant life change. Here are some strategies for supporting the emotional well-being of the outgoing leader:

11.3.1 Acknowledge and Validate Emotions

The first step in supporting emotional well-being is to acknowledge and validate the range of emotions the outgoing leader may experience. It is normal for them to feel a mix of emotions, including sadness, loss, uncertainty, and even relief. By acknowledging and validating these emotions, you create a safe space for them to express their feelings and process their experiences.

Encourage open and honest communication, allowing the outgoing leader to share their thoughts and emotions without judgment. Active listening and empathy are essential during this time. By showing understanding and compassion, you can help them feel heard and supported.

11.3.2 Provide Transition Support

Transitioning from a leadership role to retirement can be overwhelming for the outgoing leader. They may struggle with a loss of identity, a sense of purpose, and a feeling of disconnection from the business they have dedicated their life to. Providing transition support can help them navigate these challenges.

Offer resources such as retirement planning workshops, coaching, or counseling services. These resources can help the outgoing leader explore their interests, set new goals, and find a sense of purpose beyond the business. Encourage them to engage in activities that bring them joy and fulfillment, whether it be pursuing hobbies, volunteering, or spending quality time with loved ones.

11.3.3 Foster a Supportive Network

Building a supportive network is crucial for the emotional well-being of the outgoing leader. Encourage them to connect with other retired business leaders or join support groups where they can share their experiences and learn from others who have gone through similar transitions.

Family support is also essential during this time. Encourage open and honest conversations with family members about the transition and the emotions involved. By fostering a supportive family environment, you can help the outgoing leader feel understood and valued beyond their role in the business.

11.3.4 Encourage Self-Care

Self-care plays a vital role in supporting emotional well-being. Encourage the outgoing leader to prioritize self-care activities that promote relaxation, stress reduction, and overall well-being. This may include exercise, meditation, spending time in nature, or engaging in creative pursuits.

Additionally, emphasize the importance of maintaining a healthy work-life balance. Encourage them to set boundaries and create a schedule that allows for leisure time and activities they enjoy. By prioritizing self-care, the outgoing leader can better manage their emotions and adjust to their new life outside of the business.

11.3.5 Seek Professional Help if Needed

Sometimes, the emotional challenges associated with transitioning from a leadership role can be overwhelming. If the outgoing leader is struggling to cope with their emotions or experiencing symptoms of depression or anxiety, it may be necessary to seek professional help.

Encourage them to reach out to a therapist or counselor who specializes in retirement and life transitions. Professional support can provide them with the tools and strategies to navigate their emotions effectively and ensure their emotional well-being.

Supporting the emotional well-being of the outgoing leader is crucial for a successful transition and the overall health of the family business. By acknowledging their emotions, providing transition support, fostering a supportive network, encouraging self-care, and seeking professional help if needed, you can help them navigate this significant life change with resilience and find fulfillment beyond the business.

11.4 Finding Purpose Beyond Business

As the torch is passed from one generation to the next, it is essential for retiring family members to find a new sense of purpose beyond their business roles. For many, their identity and self-worth have been closely tied to their professional achievements and the success of the family business. Letting go of this identity can be a daunting task, but it is crucial for personal growth and overall well-being.

11.4.1 Embracing Personal Growth

Retirement offers a unique opportunity for individuals to explore new passions, interests, and hobbies. It is a time to rediscover oneself and embrace personal growth. Engaging in activities that bring joy and fulfillment can help retirees find a renewed sense of purpose and meaning in life. Whether it's pursuing a long-held dream, volunteering for a cause they are passionate about, or dedicating time to personal relationships, finding purpose beyond business is essential for a fulfilling retirement.

11.4.2 Mentoring and Giving Back

Retiring family members have a wealth of knowledge and experience that can be invaluable to the next generation and the wider community. Mentoring younger family members or aspiring entrepreneurs can provide a sense of fulfillment and purpose. Sharing wisdom, guiding others, and witnessing their growth can be incredibly rewarding. Additionally, getting involved in philanthropic endeavors allows retirees to give back to society and make a positive impact beyond the confines of their business.

11.4.3 Pursuing Personal Passions

Retirement provides an opportunity to pursue personal passions that may have been put on hold during the demands of running a family business. Whether it's art, music, travel, or any other interest, retirees can now dedicate time and energy to activities that bring them joy and fulfillment. Exploring these passions not only enriches their own lives but also serves as an inspiration to others, showing that life can be vibrant and fulfilling beyond the confines of work.

11.4.4 Continuity through Family Values

While retiring from the family business, family members can still play a vital role in preserving the family's values and legacy. By actively participating in family gatherings, celebrations, and events, retirees can contribute to maintaining a strong family culture. Sharing stories, traditions, and values with younger generations ensures that the family's identity and heritage are passed down through the generations. This sense of continuity can provide a deep sense of purpose and fulfillment for retirees.

11.4.5 Exploring New Business Ventures

For some retiring family members, the desire to remain involved in business may still burn strong.

Exploring new business ventures, either independently or in collaboration with the next generation, can provide a sense of purpose and fulfillment. This could involve starting a new business, investing in startups, or becoming a mentor to young entrepreneurs. By leveraging their experience and expertise, retirees can continue to make a meaningful impact in the business world while embracing a new chapter in their lives.

11.4.6 Embracing a Balanced Lifestyle

Retirement offers an opportunity to prioritize personal well-being and embrace a balanced lifestyle. This includes taking care of physical health through regular exercise, maintaining social connections, and nurturing personal relationships. By focusing on overall well-being, retirees can find a sense of purpose in living a fulfilling and meaningful life beyond the boundaries of their business.

Finding purpose beyond business is a deeply personal journey that requires self-reflection, exploration, and a willingness to embrace change. It is a process that may take time and experimentation, but the rewards are immeasurable. By letting go of the past and embracing new opportunities, retiring family members can find a renewed sense of purpose, fulfillment, and joy in their post-business lives.

Legacy Beyond Loss

12.1 Honoring Family Values and Traditions

Family businesses are often built on a foundation of strong values and traditions that have been passed down through generations. These values and traditions shape the culture and identity of the family and the business itself. As the torch is passed from one generation to the next, it becomes crucial to honor and preserve these values and traditions to maintain the family's legacy.

12.1.1 Understanding the Significance

Family values and traditions serve as guiding principles that define the purpose and direction of the business. They provide a sense of identity and belonging for family members and employees alike. Honoring these values and traditions not only ensures continuity but also fosters a sense of pride and loyalty within the family and the organization.

12.1.2 Documenting and Communicating

To effectively honor family values and traditions, it is essential to document and communicate them clearly. This can be done through a family constitution or a set of guiding principles that outline the core values and traditions of the family business. By documenting these values and traditions, they become tangible and can be shared with future generations, ensuring their preservation.

12.1.3 Leading by Example

Honoring family values and traditions starts at the top, with the current generation of leaders setting the example for the next. Leaders must embody these values and traditions in their actions and decisions, demonstrating their commitment to upholding the family's legacy. By leading by example, they inspire and motivate the next generation to carry forward these values and traditions with pride and integrity.

12.1.4 Adapting to Change

While honoring family values and traditions is crucial, it is also important to recognize that the world is constantly evolving. As the business and the family navigate through different eras and generations, there may be a need to adapt certain aspects of the values and traditions to remain relevant and competitive. This does not mean abandoning the core principles but rather finding a balance between tradition and innovation.

12.1.5 Involving the Next Generation

To ensure the continuity of family values and traditions, it is vital to involve the next generation in the process. This can be done through mentorship programs, family meetings, and open discussions about the values and traditions that define the family business. By actively involving the next generation, they develop a deeper understanding and appreciation for the values and traditions, making them more likely to carry them forward.

12.1.6 Celebrating Milestones and Rituals

One way to honor family values and traditions is by celebrating milestones and rituals that have been passed down through generations. These can include anniversaries, special events, or even simple rituals that hold significance for the family. By continuing these traditions, the family business maintains a sense of continuity and reinforces the values that have guided it throughout its history.

12.1.7 Engaging the Community

Family businesses often have deep roots within their communities. Honoring family values and traditions can extend beyond the internal dynamics of the family to include the broader community. By actively engaging with the community and supporting causes that align with the family's values, the business can create a positive impact and leave a lasting legacy beyond its own walls.

12.1.8 Seeking Professional Guidance

Navigating the complexities of honoring family values and traditions can be challenging. In some cases, seeking professional guidance from consultants or advisors who specialize in family business succession can be beneficial. These professionals can provide insights and strategies for effectively preserving and honoring the family's values and traditions while adapting to the changing business landscape.

In conclusion, honoring family values and traditions is a critical aspect of preserving the family's identity and creating a lasting impact. By understanding the significance, documenting and communicating, leading by example, adapting to change, involving the next generation, celebrating milestones and rituals, engaging the community, and seeking professional guidance, family businesses can navigate the challenges of succession while staying true to their roots.

12.2 Maintaining a Strong Family Culture

A strong family culture is the foundation upon which a successful family business is built. It encompasses the shared values, beliefs, traditions, and norms that guide the behavior and decision-making of family members within the business. Maintaining this culture is crucial for the long-term success and sustainability of the family business, as it fosters unity, loyalty, and a sense of purpose among family members.

12.2.1 Defining the Family Culture

Before we can discuss how to maintain a strong family culture, it is important to first define what it means for your specific family business. Family culture is unique to each family and is shaped by a variety of factors, including the family's history, values, and traditions. Take the time to reflect on what is important to your family and how these values can be integrated into the business.

12.2.2 Communicating and Reinforcing Values

Once the family culture has been defined, it is essential to communicate and reinforce these values throughout the organization. This can be done through regular family meetings, where family members come together to discuss and align on important decisions and values. These meetings provide an opportunity to share stories, traditions, and experiences that reinforce the family culture and create a sense of belonging.

In addition to family meetings, it is important to integrate the family culture into the day-to-day operations of the business. This can be done through the development of policies and practices that reflect the family's values and expectations. For example, if the family values transparency and open communication, implementing regular communication channels and feedback mechanisms can help reinforce these values.

12.2.3 Nurturing Relationships and Collaboration

A strong family culture is built on strong relationships and collaboration among family members. It is important to foster an environment where family members feel supported, respected, and valued. This can be achieved through team-building activities, mentorship programs, and regular family gatherings outside of the business context.

Encouraging collaboration and teamwork among family members is also crucial for maintaining a strong family culture. This can be done by creating opportunities for family members to work together on projects or initiatives, fostering a sense of shared purpose and accomplishment. By working together, family members can leverage their individual strengths and expertise to drive the success of the business.

12.2.4 Balancing Tradition and Innovation

Maintaining a strong family culture requires striking a balance between honoring tradition and embracing innovation. While tradition provides a sense of continuity and stability, innovation is necessary for the long-term growth and relevance of the business. It is important to create an environment where both tradition and innovation are valued and encouraged.

One way to achieve this balance is by involving multiple generations in the decision-making process. By including younger family members in strategic discussions and encouraging their input, you can tap into their fresh perspectives and innovative ideas while still respecting the wisdom and experience of older generations. This collaborative approach ensures that the family culture remains dynamic and adaptable to changing times.

12.2.5 Investing in Succession Planning

Maintaining a strong family culture requires a long-term perspective and investment in succession planning. Succession planning involves identifying and developing the next generation of leaders within the family business. By investing in the development of family members and providing them with the necessary skills and knowledge, you can ensure a smooth transition of leadership while preserving the family culture.

Succession planning should not be limited to the transfer of leadership roles but should also include the transfer of values, traditions, and the family culture itself. This can be achieved through mentorship programs, leadership development initiatives, and the creation of opportunities for family members to learn from one another.

12.2.6 Celebrating Milestones and Achievements

Finally, maintaining a strong family culture involves celebrating milestones and achievements as a family. Recognizing and acknowledging the contributions and successes of family members fosters a sense of pride and unity. This can be done through formal events, such as anniversary celebrations or award ceremonies, as well as informal gatherings where family members come together to share stories and memories.

By celebrating milestones and achievements, you not only reinforce the family culture but also create a sense of continuity and purpose for future generations. It serves as a reminder of the family's legacy and the importance of preserving it for generations to come.

In conclusion, maintaining a strong family culture is essential for the long-term success and sustainability of a family business. By defining and communicating the family values, nurturing relationships and collaboration, balancing tradition and innovation, investing in succession planning, and celebrating milestones and achievements, you can ensure that the family culture remains vibrant and resilient. This, in turn, will contribute to the preservation of the family's identity and the creation of a lasting legacy.

12.3 Passing on Ethical Standards

Ethics play a crucial role in the success and longevity of a family business. They serve as a guiding compass, shaping the decisions and actions of both current and future generations. As the torch is passed from one generation to the next, it becomes essential to ensure that the ethical standards established by the founding generation are preserved and upheld.

12.3.1 Instilling Values from the Start

Passing on ethical standards begins with instilling core values in the younger generation from an early age. These values should be deeply rooted in integrity, honesty, respect, and fairness. By incorporating these principles into everyday family life, children grow up understanding the importance of ethical behavior and its impact on the family business.

Parents and grandparents can lead by example, demonstrating ethical decision-making and discussing the reasoning behind their choices. Engaging in open conversations about ethical dilemmas and their potential consequences helps younger family members develop a strong moral compass.

12.3.2 Formalizing Ethical Guidelines

While instilling values is crucial, it is equally important to formalize ethical guidelines within the family business. These guidelines serve as a reference point for all family members, ensuring a consistent approach to ethical decision-making.

Creating a code of conduct or ethics policy can help articulate the family's values and expectations. This document should outline the ethical principles that guide the business, as well as the consequences for violating these standards. By establishing clear expectations, family members have a framework to navigate ethical challenges and make informed choices.

12.3.3 Leading by Example

Leadership within the family business has a significant influence on the ethical culture of the organization. As the torch is passed to the next generation, it is essential for leaders to embody the ethical standards they expect from others.

Leaders should consistently demonstrate ethical behavior, making decisions that align with the family's values and principles. By leading by example, they inspire trust and encourage others to follow suit. This not only strengthens the ethical fabric of the business but also fosters a culture of integrity and accountability.

12.3.4 Education and Training

To ensure the continuity of ethical standards, it is crucial to provide education and training opportunities for family members. This can include workshops, seminars, or even formal courses on ethics and responsible business practices.

By investing in the development of ethical leadership skills, family members gain the knowledge and tools necessary to navigate complex ethical dilemmas. These educational initiatives also provide a platform for open dialogue and the exchange of ideas, fostering a culture of continuous learning and growth.

12.3.5 Ethical Decision-Making Processes

In addition to instilling values and providing education, it is essential to establish robust ethical decision-making processes within the family business. These processes should encourage open discussion, collaboration, and the consideration of diverse perspectives.

Creating a framework for ethical decision-making helps ensure that choices are made in alignment with the family's values and principles. This can involve establishing an ethics committee or appointing an ethics officer who is responsible for overseeing ethical practices and addressing any concerns that may arise.

12.3.6 Holding Each Other Accountable

Preserving ethical standards requires a collective effort from all family members involved in the business. Holding each other accountable for upholding these standards is crucial to maintaining the family's integrity and reputation.

Regular communication and feedback sessions can provide a platform for discussing ethical concerns and addressing any deviations from the established ethical guidelines. By fostering a culture of accountability, family members can support each other in making ethical choices and ensure the long-term sustainability of the family business.

12.3.7 Philanthropy and Social Responsibility

Passing on ethical standards goes beyond the internal operations of the family business. It also extends to the family's impact on society and the environment. Engaging in philanthropic activities and embracing social responsibility initiatives can be a powerful way to demonstrate the family's commitment to ethical behavior.

By giving back to the community and supporting causes aligned with their values, the family business can create a lasting impact and inspire others to follow suit. Philanthropy and social responsibility initiatives also provide an opportunity for family members to work together towards a common goal, strengthening family bonds and the sense of purpose beyond business.

In conclusion, passing on ethical standards is a critical aspect of preserving the family's identity and ensuring the long-term success of the business. By instilling values, formalizing guidelines, leading by example, providing education and training, establishing ethical decision-making processes, holding each other accountable, and engaging in philanthropy and social responsibility, families can create a legacy that extends far beyond financial success.

12.4 Creating a Lasting Impact

Creating a lasting impact is about more than just maintaining the status quo or preserving the family's legacy. It is about actively shaping the future of the business and leaving a positive mark on the world. This section explores strategies and approaches that can help family businesses create a lasting impact that extends beyond their immediate sphere of influence.

12.4.1 Embracing Corporate Social Responsibility

One way to create a lasting impact is by embracing corporate social responsibility (CSR). CSR involves integrating social and environmental concerns into business operations and interactions with stakeholders. By actively engaging in CSR initiatives, family businesses can contribute to the well-being of their communities and the broader society.

Family businesses can identify social and environmental issues that align with their values and mission. They can then develop initiatives and programs that address these issues, such as supporting local charities, implementing sustainable practices, or providing educational opportunities for underprivileged individuals. By doing so, family businesses can leave a positive and lasting impact on the communities they serve.

12.4.2 Investing in Research and Development

To create a lasting impact, family businesses must also embrace innovation and invest in research and development (R&D). By continuously seeking new ideas, technologies, and solutions, family businesses can stay ahead of the curve and remain relevant in a rapidly changing business landscape.

Allocating resources to R&D allows family businesses to explore new markets, develop new products or services, and improve existing offerings. This commitment to innovation not only ensures the long-term viability of the business but also positions it as a leader in its industry. By creating innovative solutions that address societal challenges or meet evolving customer needs, family businesses can make a lasting impact on their industry and beyond.

12.4.3 Fostering Collaboration and Partnerships

Creating a lasting impact often requires collaboration and partnerships with external organizations, stakeholders, and even competitors. By working together, family businesses can leverage their collective resources, expertise, and networks to tackle complex issues and drive positive change.

Family businesses can seek out partnerships with non-profit organizations, academic institutions, or government agencies that share their values and goals. These collaborations can lead to joint initiatives, research projects, or advocacy campaigns that address social, environmental, or economic challenges. By pooling their resources and knowledge, family businesses can make a more significant and lasting impact than they could achieve alone.

12.4.4 Mentoring and Supporting the Next Generation

Creating a lasting impact also involves nurturing and supporting the next generation of leaders within the family business. By providing mentorship, guidance, and opportunities for growth, family businesses can ensure a smooth transition of leadership while empowering the next generation to make their mark on the business and the world.

Family businesses can establish formal mentorship programs, leadership development initiatives, or educational scholarships to support the growth and development of the next generation. By investing in their development, family businesses can equip them with the skills, knowledge, and values necessary to continue the legacy and create a lasting impact.

12.4.5 Measuring and Communicating Impact

To create a lasting impact, family businesses must also measure and communicate their impact effectively. By establishing clear metrics and evaluation frameworks, family businesses can assess the effectiveness of their initiatives and make data-driven decisions to maximize their impact.

Furthermore, family businesses should communicate their impact to stakeholders, including employees, customers, investors, and the wider community. By sharing success stories, lessons learned, and the positive outcomes of their initiatives, family businesses can inspire others and encourage collective action towards a more sustainable and inclusive future.

In conclusion, creating a lasting impact requires family businesses to embrace corporate social responsibility, invest in research and development, foster collaboration and partnerships, mentor and support the next generation, and measure and communicate their impact effectively. By taking these steps, family businesses can ensure that their legacy extends beyond their time and leaves a positive and lasting mark on the world.

The Third-Generation Challenge

13.1 Recognizing the Third-Generation Syndrome

The third generation of a family business often faces unique challenges that can hinder the continuity and growth of the enterprise. This phenomenon, known as the "Third-Generation Syndrome," refers to the difficulties that arise when the business is passed down to the grandchildren of the founder. While the first and second generations may have successfully navigated the initial stages of succession, the third generation often struggles to maintain the same level of success. In this section, we will explore the reasons behind this syndrome and discuss strategies for overcoming its negative effects.

13.1.1 The Cycle of Entitlement and Complacency

One of the primary factors contributing to the Third-Generation Syndrome is the sense of entitlement that can develop among family members who have grown up with the privileges and benefits of the business. The third generation may have witnessed the success of their parents and grandparents without fully understanding the hard work and sacrifices that went into building the business. As a result, they may feel entitled to the same level of success without putting in the necessary effort.

This entitlement can lead to complacency, as third-generation family members may become less motivated to innovate and adapt to changing market conditions. They may rely on the reputation and past achievements of the business, rather than actively seeking new opportunities for growth. This complacency can be detrimental to the long-term success of the business, as it hinders the ability to stay competitive in a rapidly evolving marketplace.

13.1.2 Fostering Entrepreneurship and Innovation

To break the cycle of entitlement and complacency, it is crucial to foster a culture of entrepreneurship and innovation within the third generation. This involves instilling a sense of ownership and responsibility for the future of the business, as well as encouraging a mindset of continuous learning and adaptation.

One way to foster entrepreneurship is by providing opportunities for family members to gain experience outside of the family business. This could involve internships or employment in other companies or industries, allowing them to develop new skills and perspectives. Exposure to different environments can help broaden their horizons and encourage innovative thinking.

Additionally, creating a supportive environment that encourages risk-taking and experimentation can help stimulate entrepreneurial behavior. This can be achieved by establishing a culture that values and rewards creativity, initiative, and calculated risk-taking. Encouraging family members to pursue their own business ventures, even if they are separate from the family business, can also foster a spirit of entrepreneurship.

13.1.3 Preparing for the Next Transition

Recognizing the challenges associated with the third generation is the first step towards overcoming them. It is essential to start planning for the next transition early on to ensure a smooth handover of leadership and responsibilities. This includes identifying and developing potential successors within the family or considering external leadership options.

To prepare the next generation for leadership roles, it is crucial to provide them with the necessary training and mentorship. This can involve formal leadership development programs, educational opportunities, and exposure to different aspects of the business. By equipping them with the skills and knowledge needed to lead, the third generation can be better prepared to break the cycle of the Third-Generation Syndrome.

Furthermore, it is important to establish clear expectations and performance metrics for family members involved in the business. This helps ensure that they are held accountable for their actions and contributions, regardless of their familial ties. By setting high standards and promoting a merit-based culture, the third generation can be motivated to strive for excellence and avoid falling into the trap of entitlement and complacency.

In conclusion, the Third-Generation Syndrome presents unique challenges that can hinder the continuity and growth of family businesses. Recognizing the cycle of entitlement and complacency is crucial in breaking this cycle and fostering a culture of entrepreneurship and innovation. By preparing the next generation for leadership roles and establishing clear expectations, family businesses can overcome the Third-

Generation Syndrome and ensure a successful transition to the next generation.

13.2 Overcoming Entitlement and Complacency

The third generation of a family business often faces a significant challenge in breaking free from the sense of entitlement and complacency that can develop over time. As the business passes from one generation to the next, there is a risk that the younger generation may take their position for granted, assuming that success is guaranteed simply because they are part of the family.

13.2.1 Recognizing the Dangers of Entitlement

Entitlement can be a silent killer of family businesses. When individuals feel entitled to their position and the benefits that come with it, they may become complacent and fail to put in the necessary effort and dedication to sustain and grow the business. This sense of entitlement can lead to a lack of innovation, a resistance to change, and a decline in overall performance.

Recognizing the dangers of entitlement is the first step in overcoming it. The third generation must understand that they have a responsibility to earn their place in the business and contribute to its success. They must recognize that entitlement can undermine their own potential and the future of the business.

13.2.2 Cultivating a Growth Mindset

To overcome entitlement and complacency, the third generation must cultivate a growth mindset. This mindset is characterized by a belief that abilities and intelligence can be developed through dedication and hard work. By adopting a growth mindset, individuals are more likely to embrace challenges, persist in the face of setbacks, and see effort as a path to mastery.

Encouraging a growth mindset within the family business involves fostering a culture of continuous learning and improvement. This can be achieved through mentorship programs, professional development opportunities, and a focus on personal and professional growth. By instilling a growth mindset, the third generation can break free from the limitations of entitlement and embrace a mindset of innovation and progress.

13.2.3 Embracing Entrepreneurship and Innovation

One effective way to overcome entitlement and complacency is to foster entrepreneurship and innovation within the family business. Encouraging the third generation to think creatively, take risks, and explore new opportunities can inject fresh energy and ideas into the business.

Creating an environment that supports entrepreneurship and innovation involves providing the necessary resources, such as access to capital, technology, and networks. It also requires a willingness to embrace change and adapt to new market trends and customer demands. By empowering the third generation to be entrepreneurial and innovative, the family business can stay competitive and relevant in an ever-evolving business landscape.

13.2.4 Preparing for the Next Transition

While the third generation focuses on overcoming entitlement and complacency, it is crucial to simultaneously prepare for the next transition. Succession planning should be an ongoing process that involves identifying and developing future leaders within the family and the business.

Preparing for the next transition requires open and honest communication among family members and stakeholders. It involves setting clear expectations, defining roles and responsibilities, and providing the necessary training and support for the next generation to step into leadership positions.

Additionally, it is essential to seek external expertise and guidance to ensure a smooth transition. Engaging professional advisors, such as lawyers, accountants, and business consultants, can provide valuable insights and help navigate the complexities of succession planning.

By actively addressing entitlement and complacency, fostering entrepreneurship and innovation, and preparing for the next transition, the third generation can break free from the cycle of stagnation and ensure the long-term success and sustainability of the family business.

In the next chapter, we will conclude our exploration of family business succession by charting a course for lasting legacies. We will discuss the importance of maintaining family values, preserving the family's identity, and leaving a lasting impact beyond the business itself.

13.3 Fostering Entrepreneurship and Innovation

As a family business enters its third generation, it often faces a critical juncture. The founders' entrepreneurial spirit and drive may have propelled the business to success, but maintaining that momentum can be a daunting task for the next generation. The third generation must find ways to break free from the cycle of complacency and entitlement that can hinder innovation and growth. Fostering entrepreneurship and innovation becomes crucial for the long-term sustainability of the family business.

13.3.1 Embracing a Culture of Innovation

To foster entrepreneurship and innovation within the family business, it is essential to create a culture that values and encourages new ideas. This starts with leadership setting the tone and actively promoting a mindset of innovation. By embracing a culture of innovation, family members are encouraged to think outside the box, challenge the status quo, and explore new opportunities.

Encouraging an entrepreneurial mindset involves providing family members with the freedom to experiment and take calculated risks. This can be achieved by creating a safe space for innovation, where failures are seen as learning opportunities rather than mistakes. By celebrating both successes and failures, the family business can cultivate an environment that fosters creativity and encourages entrepreneurial thinking.

13.3.2 Nurturing Entrepreneurial Skills

Nurturing entrepreneurial skills within the third generation is crucial for the future success of the family business. This involves providing family members with the necessary education, training, and mentorship to develop their entrepreneurial capabilities. Offering opportunities for formal education in entrepreneurship or business management can equip family members with the knowledge and skills needed to drive innovation.

In addition to formal education, it is essential to provide practical experiences that allow family members to apply their entrepreneurial skills. This can include internships or rotational programs within the family business or even encouraging family members to gain external work experience to broaden their perspectives. By exposing them to different industries and business models, family members can gain valuable insights and bring fresh ideas back to the family business.

13.3.3 Creating an Innovation Ecosystem

To foster entrepreneurship and innovation, it is crucial to create an ecosystem that supports and nurtures new ideas. This can involve establishing innovation labs or incubators within the family business, where family members can collaborate and experiment with new concepts. These spaces can serve as a hub for creativity, providing resources, mentorship, and a supportive network for aspiring entrepreneurs within the family.

In addition to internal innovation initiatives, family businesses can also explore external partnerships and collaborations. By engaging with startups, universities, or industry experts, family businesses can tap into external sources of innovation and gain fresh perspectives. These collaborations can lead to the development of new products, services, or business models that can drive growth and ensure the family business remains competitive in a rapidly changing business landscape.

13.3.4 Embracing Technology and Digital Transformation

In today's digital age, embracing technology and digital transformation is crucial for the long-term success of any business, including family businesses. The third generation must be open to adopting new technologies and leveraging digital tools to drive innovation and improve operational efficiency. This can involve investing in digital infrastructure, implementing data analytics, or exploring emerging technologies such as artificial intelligence or blockchain.

By embracing technology, family businesses can streamline processes, enhance customer experiences, and identify new market opportunities. It also allows for greater agility and adaptability, enabling the family business to respond to changing customer demands and market trends. Embracing technology and digital transformation can be a catalyst for innovation and growth within the family business.

Conclusion

Fostering entrepreneurship and innovation within a family business is essential for its long-term success and sustainability. By creating a culture of innovation, nurturing entrepreneurial skills, creating an innovation ecosystem, and embracing technology, the third generation can break free from the cycle of complacency and drive the family business forward. By embracing change and fostering a spirit of entrepreneurship, the family business can adapt to the evolving business landscape and continue to thrive for generations to come.

13.4 Preparing for the Next Transition

As the third generation prepares to take the reins of the family business, it is crucial to approach the next transition with careful planning and foresight. The challenges faced by third-generation family members are often distinct from those of previous generations, as they must navigate the delicate balance between honoring tradition and embracing innovation. In this section, we will discuss the key considerations and strategies for preparing for the next transition.

13.4.1 Defining the Vision and Direction

Before embarking on the next transition, it is essential to define a clear vision and direction for the future of the family business. This involves engaging in open and honest discussions with family members to understand their aspirations, goals, and values. By aligning the vision of the third generation with the legacy of the previous generations, it becomes easier to create a roadmap for the future.

13.4.2 Identifying and Developing Next-Generation Leaders

One of the critical factors in ensuring a successful transition is identifying and developing the next generation of leaders within the family. This involves assessing the skills, strengths, and interests of family members and providing them with the necessary training and development opportunities. By nurturing their leadership capabilities, the family business can ensure a smooth transition and continuity of success.

13.4.3 Embracing Innovation and Adaptability

In today's rapidly changing business landscape, it is crucial for family businesses to embrace innovation and adaptability. The third generation must be open to new ideas, technologies, and market trends. By fostering a culture of innovation and encouraging entrepreneurial thinking, the family business can stay relevant and competitive in the long run.

13.4.4 Establishing Effective Governance Structures

To ensure the smooth transition and continued success of the family business, it is essential to establish effective governance structures. This involves defining clear roles and responsibilities, implementing transparent decision-making processes, and establishing mechanisms for resolving conflicts. By creating a robust governance framework, the family business can navigate the complexities of succession and maintain harmony within the family.

13.4.5 Building a Strong Support Network

Preparing for the next transition requires building a strong support network both within and outside the family. This includes engaging with external advisors, such as consultants, lawyers, and accountants, who can provide objective guidance and expertise. Additionally, fostering strong relationships with industry peers and associations can offer valuable insights and networking opportunities.

13.4.6 Communicating and Managing Expectations

Effective communication and managing expectations are crucial during the transition process. It is essential to have open and honest conversations with family members about their roles, responsibilities, and expectations. By setting clear expectations and maintaining open lines of communication, the family business can minimize misunderstandings and conflicts.

13.4.7 Continuously Evaluating and Adjusting the Plan

Preparing for the next transition is an ongoing process that requires continuous evaluation and adjustment. As the business landscape evolves, it is crucial to reassess the strategic plan and make necessary adjustments to ensure its relevance and effectiveness. Regularly reviewing the plan and seeking feedback from family members and key stakeholders can help identify areas for improvement and drive continuous growth.

In conclusion, preparing for the next transition in a family business is a complex and multifaceted process. By defining a clear vision, identifying, and developing next-generation leaders, embracing innovation, establishing effective governance structures, building a strong support network, communicating and managing expectations, and continuously evaluating and adjusting the plan, the family business can navigate the challenges and ensure a successful transition. The third generation has the opportunity to break the cycle and create a lasting legacy for future generations to come.

Charting the Course for Lasting Legacies

As we draw the curtains on this exploration into the intricate landscape of family business succession, we find ourselves standing at the juncture of the past, present, and the uncharted territories of the future. The journey has been one of introspection, revelation, and the unveiling of the silent struggles that accompany the transition of generations in family businesses.

Reflecting on Silent Suffering:

We began by delving into the depths of silent suffering, unveiling the emotional complexities that shroud succession. The struggles of letting go, the weight of expectations, and the profound impact on personal identity—these tribulations form the undercurrents that often go unnoticed. By shedding light on these emotional landscapes, we acknowledged the profound humanity inherent in the process of passing the torch.

Navigating the Unseen Burden:

Our exploration continued to the unseen burden of generational transition, where power dynamics, succession planning challenges, and the delicate fabric of family relationships came to the forefront. The discussion aimed not only to expose these challenges but also to offer strategies for navigating these turbulent waters, fostering collaboration, and nurturing the bonds that transcend generations.

Balancing Tradition and Innovation:

The legacy conundrum posed yet another challenge—how to balance tradition and innovation. Preserving the family legacy while embracing change and adaptation requires a delicate dance, and our examination aimed to unravel the intricacies of finding this equilibrium. We explored the preparation paradox, underscoring the significance of early planning, leadership transition, and resilience in the face of unexpected events.

Bridging the Generational Chasm:

The generational chasm, a common stumbling block in family businesses, became a focal point. Our exploration offered insights into understanding generational differences, fostering effective communication, building trust, and mitigating common pitfalls that often impede the seamless flow of ideas and values between generations.

The Professional Pivot:

As we navigated the professional pivot, we considered the complexities of hiring external leaders versus nurturing internal talent. The discussion provided guidance on developing and retaining internal talent, crafting effective leadership development programs, and preparing emotionally for farewells.

Preserving Identity Beyond Loss:

Preserving the family's identity emerged as a poignant theme, delving into the importance of honoring values and traditions, cultivating a strong family culture, and passing on ethical standards. We confronted the challenges faced by the third generation, offering strategies to overcome entitlement and complacency, foster entrepreneurship, and prepare for the next transition.

Charting the Course Forward:

Now, armed with the knowledge gained from the trials and triumphs of family businesses, we embark on charting a course for lasting legacies. This conclusion serves not as an end but as a beginning— a roadmap for readers to navigate the intricate and sometimes turbulent waters of family business succession. May this journey inspire resilience, collaboration, and a profound commitment to preserving the heritage and success of your family business.

As you navigate the complexities of succession, may the wisdom within these pages guide you, the shared experiences resonate with you, and the strategies empower you to build a lasting legacy—a legacy that transcends time and stands as a testament to the enduring power of family businesses.

with immense gratitude

Robert Jhonson

Summary

www.ingramcontent.com/pod-product-compliance
Lightning Source LLC
Chambersburg PA
CBHW050446290526
45786CB00006B/2185